Creative
Church
Administration

Creative
Church
Administration

Lyle E. Schaller and
Charles A. Tidwell

ABINGDON
NASHVILLE

CREATIVE CHURCH ADMINISTRATION
Copyright © 1975 by Abingdon Press

Library of Congress Cataloging in Publication Data

Schaller, Lyle E.
Creative Church Administration.
    Bibliography: p.
    1. Church management. I. Tidwell, Charles A.,
joint author. II. Title.
        BV652.S28   254   75-15953

ISBN 0-687-09816-5

Scripture quotations noted RSV are from the Revised
Standard Version of the Bible, copyrighted 1946, 1952, and
1971 by the Division of Christian Education, National
Council of Churches, and are used by permission.

Scripture quotations noted Williams are from *The New
Testament: A Private Translation in the Language
of the People* by Charles B. Williams. Copyright, 1937,
by Bruce Humphries, Inc. Copyright assigned, 1949, to the
Moody Bible Institute of Chicago.

Portions of this book are based on material which first appeared elsewhere. Grateful acknowledgment is made to the
following periodicals:

The Lutheran, for "Learn from Others" (February 21,
1973). Copyright 1973 by *The Lutheran,* magazine of the
Lutheran Church in America. Reprinted by permission.

Presbyterian Survey, for "Where Are the Young Marrieds?"
(February, 1975). Copyright 1975 by *Presbyterian Survey.*
Reprinted by permission.

MANUFACTURED BY THE PARTHENON PRESS AT
NASHVILLE, TENNESSEE, UNITED STATES OF AMERICA

Contents

Introduction

Why another book on church administration?

In responding to that question it may be helpful first to review the changing emphases in church administration since the turn of the century.

The first books to be published on church administration can be described simply as sharing experiences. They are to church administration, as we know it today, what reminiscences and autobiographies are to history.

The value of these early efforts to systematize the experiences of a "successful" pastor should not be dismissed lightly, however. Their authors made several significant contributions, among them the sharing of "lessons from experience," the recognition that there were skills that could be transmitted from one person to another, and the focusing of attention on another dimension of the minister's work in addition to the traditional responsibilities of preaching, visitation, and evangelism.

An examination of these books reveals that they tended to be based on a task-oriented approach. They were directed at pastors serving in congregations organized around a series of semi-independent and largely self-contained groups such as the Sunday school, the Ladies' Aid, a youth organization, a men's club, and similar subgroups.

The subject matter was confined largely to church finances and raising money, increasing church attendance, working with a church board, organizing an office, the use of equipment, program ideas, staff relationships, and public relations.

Without exception the authors projected a concept of the traditional leadership pyramid with the pastor sitting in the seat at the top. (Since most of these books were written before I was born, I lack a first-hand knowledge of the situation, but I have a hunch that in many congregations the pastor sat in the seat at the top of the leadership pyramid on public display, while a layman occupied the seat in the less visible leadership pyramid that represented reality.)

Beginning a little later and overlapping this group of task-oriented books on church administration came a seemingly endless series on "leadership training." That term has since been applied to so many different concepts of administration that anyone using it today should follow it up immediately with a two-or three-paragraph definition of what he means by those words. The earlier authors, however, were reasonably clear on what they meant by leadership training. As Frederick A. Agar, one of the most prolific and concise of these men wrote: "This little book undertakes to deal with the training of lay leaders for the task of the Church. As the United States army needed a Plattsburg for the training of her officers, so does the Church need trained lay leaders to lead her forces to victory." Other writers concentrated their efforts on such specialized tasks as evangelism, church finances, preaching, and the Sunday school.

One of the major themes that ran through both the books on church administration in general and the volumes on specific functions was the importance of efficiency. Whether this was a cause of or a response to the emphasis on efficiency in public education it is impossible to say with absolute assurance. My guess, however, is that it was a reflection of what was being said and written in educational administration, where some remarkable standards were being developed to measure the "efficiency" of a school system.

In summary, the literature on church administration of

the first three decades of this century reflected an emphasis on tasks, on efficiency, on the value of organization, and on the minister as the center of the local ecclesiastical circle.

During the next three decades most of the books in the field tended to parallel the approach, style, and emphasis of the first third of the century. There were, however, five significant additions to this stream.

The first—and possibly the first book that can be said to mark a major watershed in church administration—was written by William H. Leach. In *Church Administration* (Nashville: Cokesbury Press, 1931) he made two major contributions. First, he recognized that the local church was founded around worship and education, and that administrative practices were geared to functions, not organization or execution. Second, he argued for a holistic approach to local church programming. In doing this he was thirty or forty years ahead of most of his supporters, but he helped to prepare the ground for one of today's most important concepts in local church administration, one that thus far has received its greatest support from persons trained in Christian education.

A second important addition to the basic concepts undergirding the discipline was a recognition of the local church as an organization. This contrasts with the earlier view of the local church as a cluster of more or less unrelated and semi-independent organizations. It reflects both Leach's emphasis on a holistic approach and also the changing nature of the local church in American culture.

Perhaps the most highly visible—and also the least valuable—addition to the general subject of church administration was the adaptation of the Madison Avenue advertising approach to presenting the Christian gospel. The beginnings of this trend go back to before 1930, and the best-known example of it was Bruce Barton's interpretation of Jesus as a model of the successful businessman and salesman.

A fourth addition to the traditional pattern was the publication of a number of books by laymen with specific administrative skills who were suggesting how the methods, techniques, and wisdom that had been accumulated in business could be utilized by the churches. While these were not the first contributions by laymen to the written literature on church administration, they tended to be written from a base of administrative skill rather than simply from enthusiasm and personal experience.

The fifth and unquestionably the most important addition made to the stream of books on church administration during this thirty-five-year period consisted of a large number of volumes that shifted the emphasis from the organization to the people. This group can be divided into two categories. In the smaller one the emphasis is on identifying groups of people with common characteristics, such as the elderly, youth, young married couples, young adults, and the divorced or the widowed.

The larger category consists of a flood of books on the dynamics of groups, the character of the small group, and interpersonal relationships. It is difficult to overstate the impact this literature has had on the life, vitality, and value system of the local church. It is also difficult to overstate the impact this school of thought has had and is having on church administration. Incidentally, some of the best books in this field have been published since 1965, by such persons as Clyde Reid, Robert C. Leslie, Mary Alice Douty, and Carl Rogers.

Since 1965 three major additions have been made to the study of church administration. The best of the three, Alvin J. Lindgren's *Foundations for Purposeful Church Administration* (Nashville: Abingdon Press, 1965), combines an emphasis on people and interpersonal relationships with an understanding of administration as a process rather than a task, and sets all this within the context of the Christian faith and the call to the church to be in mission.

The newest of the three is *To Come Alive!* by James D. Anderson (New York: Harper & Row, 1973). This is a pioneering effort by an Episcopal priest to adapt the concepts of organizational development to congregational renewal.

The most difficult to read of the three was written by a Church of England clergyman from Tasmania. In this volume, *Ministry and Management: Studies in Ecclesiastical Administration* (London: Tavistock Publications, 1968), Peter Rudge combines the insights of public administration with a solid theological perception of the church and offers today's church leader a base for utilizing many of the insights and methods of contemporary administration. This book represents the best effort thus far to adapt the methods and skills of public and business administration to church administration. Between these three volumes and the books on church administration published before 1960 is a gulf comparable to the difference between the DC-3 and the 747.

Running against this current has been a growing tide of sentiment which is critical of any effort to use "business" procedures in the churches. Much of this criticism can be reduced to five negative comments.

The first is an echo of Pelagianism. Pelagius, a British monk, came to Rome near the end of the fourth century and saw a pressing need for reform. He argued that man was given the degree of free will sufficient to fulfill his obligations to God and need only exert himself to do so. The Pelagians denied that the taint of Adam's sin had been transmitted to all Adam's descendants. The concept that man is a moral person and is able to follow God's will if he only chooses to act in a moral manner was declared heretical by the Council of Ephesus in 431. The contemporary Pelagians in the churches often contend that through the use of scientific management practices the worshiping congregation can be a completely faithful servant of God. This book is based on a very strong affirmation of the doctrine of original sin, and much of it is based on the assumption that structures and organizations created and managed by sinful people tend to undermine the individual's and the congregation's attempts to be faithful and obedient to the call of God.

13

The second criticism is that good management practices in the churches tend to be counterproductive. This point has some validity in that all too often the emphasis on management does tend to close doors to the Holy Spirit and to be counterproductive in the long run. This criticism is less significant for those who believe in the orthodox Christian doctrine of the universality of sin, who are convinced that God is at work in the world today, and who recognize that planning never solves problems but only means trading one set of problems for a different set. One response to this dilemma can be found on pages 58-62.

The third criticism is that good management practices in the churches are too complex and that everything should be kept very simple. When translated into operational English this criticism suggests that the goal should be to become less sensitive to the needs of people. It is a truism that the more sensitive an organization is to the needs of people, the more complex will be its operation. Jesus repeatedly encountered people who sought a simple road to salvation.

The fourth of these contemporary criticisms has real validity and underscores the importance of the concept of the universality of sin. Too often good management practices begin as a means to an end and soon become an end in themselves (the balanced church budget is a very common example of this). When looked at seriously, however, this is not really a criticism of good management practices. Poor administrative practices also become canonized. The use of average attendance, rather than qualitative factors, in evaluating the Sunday school is perhaps the most common example of this. There is persuasive evidence that not only do quantity and quality not go together in the Sunday school, but they actually appear to be incompatible. The problem identified by this criticism is real, but the source of the problem lies in the sinful nature of man and of the institutions he creates, not in administrative and management practices, good or bad.

The last of these five criticisms is the most frivolous. It is commonly expressed in these words: "The emphasis on good administrative practices may be all right for General Motors, but the church is not General Motors!" The second half of that statement is true, but simply because General Motors or IBM places a high premium on good administration does not mean the churches should place a very low value on administration. Should the churches also stop using electricity, paper, filmstrips, or enclosed buildings simply because these are used by secular organizations?

It is within this historical and critical context that this volume should be examined. Our intention is to emphasize creativity. The first chapter is based on the assumption that creativity is influenced by the frame of reference church leaders carry around with them and by the organizational context. Most of this initial chapter is devoted to suggesting how the organizational structure can be altered to increase participation, enthusiasm, creativity, widespread ownership of goals, and openness to innovation. The second chapter is based on the assumption that the leaders in every congregation attempt to plan, but that too often the planning model used sets up a self-defeating process. Several different planning models are discussed in this chapter, and the merits of flexibility are emphasized.

The third chapter is a response to the plea spoken most often by church leaders—"How do we motivate people?" This is followed by a chapter directed at the enlistment of people. This fourth chapter is directed toward the identification and development of volunteers for leadership and emphasizes the need for a continuing process including support of volunteer leaders after they have assumed leadership roles.

One of the most effective methods of encouraging creativity is to listen and to learn from others. Two approaches for this are described in the fifth chapter. The first is how to elicit the hopes, dreams, and wishes of the members. The second is how to learn from the experiences of other congregations in other places.

15

A plan for ministry is an essential element of creative church administration, and the nature, values, and process of developing a church ministries plan constitute the sixth chapter.

Perhaps the major issue facing thousands of long-established congregations is how to reach a new generation of people, and also the millions of church members who have "dropped out of church," with the Good News of Jesus Christ. This is the subject of the seventh chapter.

Three issues which most often occupy a large amount of time for those concerned with church administration are setting the salary for the minister for the coming year, financing capital improvements, and the use of the building. These three subjects are discussed in chapters 8, 9, and 10.

An essential element of church administration is evaluation, a process which traditionally has been highly dependent on the use of quantitative measurements. Several approaches to building qualitative measurements into the evaluation process are discussed in the last chapter.

Occasionally the reader of a book with more than one author inquires as to who wrote which parts of the volume. This is a fair question, and in this case it is also an easy one to answer. This introduction and chapters 1, 2, 5, 7, the first half of 8, and 10 and 11 were written by Schaller, while Tidwell is the author of chapters 3, 4, 6, the second half of 8, and all of chapter 9.

Together we hope that the reader will find it helpful and also consistent with the emerging emphases in church administration to be more sensitive to the differences among people, to be conscious of the blighting impact of institutional pressures, to avoid self-defeating behavior, to be more conscious of the call to be faithful and obedient than of the call to be "successful," and to be ever mindful that church administration is God-centered, Spirit-led, and person-oriented.

What Are Your Values?

As reflected in the actions and administrative processes, what are the values expressed in your congregation? Which is given the higher value, creativity or verbal skills? Tradition or innovation? Ministry or money? Representation of the optimum number of groups and organizations, or performance? Care of people or care of property? Responsible, representative church government, or personal satisfactions? Distributing scarce leadership talents fairly among an excess of needs, or encouraging self-motivation?

If you will examine the internal communication system and the "reward system" in your congregation, you will be able to identify many of the values of your church as an organization. Only after doing this will you be able to encourage creativity in the processes for planning, decision-making, and administration in the worshiping congregation.

It may be helpful to look at several different dimensions of congregational life to illustrate this concept.

The frame of reference used by the members, the manner in which the congregation is organized, the method for nominating individuals for leadership positions, the process for formulating goals, the structure for allocating financial resources, and the "reward system" will determine the boundaries for creativity within that institutional expression of the universal church which we identify as the worshiping congregation.

What Is Your Frame of Reference?

Perhaps the best way to begin is to examine the frame of reference used by the members in communicating with one another and with nonmembers about the nature, the values, and the priorities of your parish. This can be illustrated by these two conversations.

Two close friends who had not seen each other for several months met for lunch one day. "How's your family?" inquired the first. "Well, I have both good news and bad news to report," replied the second man. "Our son Jim is finishing the work on his master's degree and already has a good job lined up with an engineering firm. Our daughter Ruth called last night to congratulate us on the fact that in seven months my wife and I will become grandparents for the first time. The bad news is that our son Ken, who hurt his knee playing football last fall, will probably walk with a limp for the rest of his life. My wife went back to work a couple of years ago with United Airlines, but if the energy crisis gets any worse she will be one of the next to be laid off."

On a different day in a different community two other close friends who had not seen each other for several months met for lunch. "You've always been an active churchman, Don—how are things going over at St. Paul's?" inquired the first. "Well, we've had some good news and some bad news," replied the second. "Church attendance is up, and last year was the best in the history of this congregation in financial terms. On the bad news side, Sunday school attendance is continuing to drop, our minister announced last Sunday that he will be leaving us in June, and the trustees tell us the time has come to put a new roof on the building and that'll cost us a chunk of money."

In both these conversations the second man used a complex frame of reference in replying to what appears to be a simple question. In fact, however, a question about the condition of "your family" or "your church" is difficult to respond to meaningfully unless the vague term "family" or

18

"church" is broken down into components. In the first conversation the speaker defined "family" in terms of his wife and three children. In the second conversation the response to the inquiry about "your church" was in the five frequently used categories: worship attendance, finances, Sunday school, minister, and building. In both conversations an additional evaluative dimension was added in terms of "good news" and "bad news."

What is the frame of reference, or the set of categories, used by members in your congregation as they talk about the church? Are the categories helpful in communicating the purpose, role, and mission of your congregation? Or do the most widely used categories overlook vital functions of the church? Is the most widely used frame of reference for looking at your congregation one which stimulates creative thinking about mission and ministry? Or does the most widely used frame of reference focus largely on the "institutional health" of the congregation?

In looking at this issue the natural inclination is to look at "them" and wonder why "they" fail to place more emphasis on such matters as the spiritual growth of the members, the outreach of the church into the community, the relationship of this congregation to the mission of the universal church around the world, evangelism, the nurturing of the love of God and the love of neighbor, the act of worship, the promotion of social and racial justice, and the care of the lonely and the downtrodden.

A more creative approach is to ask, "What have we, the leaders of the congregation and of the denomination, done or not done which has encouraged both the laity and the clergy to develop the frame of reference they use in looking at their congregations? Have we done something which has tended to stifle creativity and to encourage a survival perspective?"

This latter approach focuses attention on that point where the leaders have control, their own decisions and actions, and thus enables them to influence the future.

19

How Did It Happen?

Why do so many people describe what is happening in their congregation in terms of the building, the minister, the number of people attending corporate worship on Sunday morning, the condition of the finances, the attendance of the Sunday school?

One large part of the answer to that question is that traditionally these five components in the life of the parish have been given the greatest visibility. Ever notice how much of the "church news" in the newspaper is devoted to building programs, a change of pastors, a special contest to boost Sunday school attendance, a guest preacher, or a special fund-raising drive? In some congregations these five areas of church life also account for most of the special communications to the members, for many of the occasions when members gather together, and for much of the organizational structure of the parish.

A second part of the reason why these five areas of church life dominate the thinking of so many members is that much of the reporting system, to both the members and the denomination, lifts up these five concerns.

A third part of the reason for the widespread use of these five categories is that all five reflect a survival perspective, and survival is a strong pressure in every institution and organization.

A fourth part of the answer is that most institutions tend to ignore or smother creativity and innovative ideas rather than to reward them. Only a few congregations are an exception to this generalization.

The frame of reference or the categories used by people in reflecting on the life and ministry of the church influences both the setting and the evaluation of goals.

For example, in many congregations the emphasis on the building as one of the categories used in looking at the church has helped produce the goal "Let's make sure that the building is in use seven days a week." (See chapter 10 for a more extended discussion of this point.) If ministry to residents of the community, rather than the building, were one of the basic categories used by members in reflecting on their church, this might have produced the goal "Let's increase our person-to-person contacts with the people now living near our meeting place."

Likewise, the use of "Sunday school," rather than the more nebulous "Christian education," has encouraged the expenditure of funds for buildings rather than for recruiting and training leaders in Christian education. The evaluation process tends to focus on the quality of the Sunday school facilities and on the average attendance rather than on giving greater support and more visibility to the various Christian education ventures carried out during the week.

If the categories people use in thinking about the church do influence expectations, goals, and the evaluation process, what can be done about it?

The obvious solution is to change the categories and encourage the development of a new frame of reference for looking at the church.

One common example familiar to many church leaders has been the congregation which accepted part or all of the financial support of a missionary or special outreach project and gave high visibility to this dimension of the total ministry of the congregation.

Another example is Christ the Redeemer Evangelical Church, a new LCA mission in suburban Cleveland, Ohio, which from its earliest days has encouraged the members to think of their parish in terms of (1) nurturing mission, (2) enabling mission, (3) serving mission, and (4) communicating mission.

The Mt. Comfort United Methodist Church, a century-old rural-turning-exurban congregation in Indiana, uses these three categories to express the purpose of the congregation: (1) congregational care, (2) outreach and evangelism, and (3) Christian social responsibility.

What are the categories you use in communicating the

21

purpose of your church to the members of your congregation? How does this influence their frame of reference? [1]

How Is Your Congregation Organized?

The same point can be illustrated by looking at how the congregation is organized for self-government purposes. Not only may the way your congregation is organized reflect a value system and a set of priorities, *but frequently the organizational structure controls the value system and sets the priorities!*

The natural, normal, and predictable sequence in organizations managed by sinful human beings is, (1) to create an organization to carry out prescribed purposes and to achieve desired goals, (2) to shift the emphasis gradually to give the highest priority to the maintenance and survival of that organization, and (3) to stifle the initiative and creativity of participating individuals in this process. For centuries institutions have been created to serve people, and before long the people become the servants of the institution, devoting most of their time and energy to the care and feeding of the institution which was created to be a servant and now has become the master. This sequence has been followed in thousands of Christian congregations.

How can this cycle be broken? How can you create a more favorable organizational climate for creativity in your congregation? How can you change the priorities back to reflecting purpose rather than institutional maintenance? How can you open the doors to creativity in the life of your congregation? One approach is to begin by looking at the values reflected in the organizational structure of your congregation.

Perhaps the easiest way of introducing the subject is to

[1] Additional dimensions of the frame of reference used by people in looking at the Christian church can be found in Lyle E. Schaller, *The Decision-Makers* (Nashville: Abingdon Press), pp. 44-62.

listen in on part of a discussion which reveals several different values and priorities reflected by different approaches to church government and congregational organization.

"There are eighty-four members on our board, but we seldom have more than fifty at any of our monthly meetings," commented a member from the First Christian (Disciples of Christ) Church.   *a.*

"When we formed our long-range planning committee we tried to include representation from every segment, point of view, faction, and interest group in the congregation," offered a member from St. John's United Church of Christ.   *b.*

"Our sixteen-member vestry has responsibility for calling the rector, setting and raising the budget, and the general oversight of the parish," stated a member from St. Paul's Episcopal Church.   *c.*

"In our parish the church council is clearly understood to be the governing body for the parish. Our council gets things done, but not everyone is always happy with every decision," added a member from St. Mark's Lutheran Church.   *d.*

"I guess we have two governing boards," commented a United Methodist member and one of two women in the group. "We have a seventy-member administrative board which apparently is based on the hope for a broad participation base, and a twenty-member council of ministries which is based on representation of all program areas and concerns. Because of its composition and smaller size it really is the power center in our congregation!"   *e.*

"I'm not sure I understand everything you folks are saying," commented a forty-year-old man from Trinity Church. "All I know is that at Trinity you have to be a member for at least ten years before you can be an usher, and you have to be an usher for at least five years before you can be elected to the board. The only exception to that is if your father and grandfather were both on the   *f.*

board you can be elected to the board by the time you're thirty and after only three or four years as an usher."

"At First Baptist we have a preacher who believes in visitation evangelism," commented a young man from that Southern Baptist congregation. "Shortly after this new preacher arrived about two years ago he preached a great sermon on the 'Great Commission.' The point I remember most vividly is that during that sermon he declared that beginning with this new program he was introducing our church would have only two kinds of members, 'Calling Baptists' and 'Chicken Baptists.' Our whole church is now organized around a program of visitation-evangelism. Our best leaders and the most prestigious jobs are concentrated in that calling program. Last year we had more baptisms than in the previous six years combined."

"As you all know, in our church the session is the governing body for the congregation," commented the member from Westminster Presbyterian Church. "Presbyterians have always operated with a system of responsible representative church government. We place a great emphasis on the apostle Paul's injunction that 'all things should be done decently and in order,' and our whole system of church courts is based on that premise."

"We completely restructured the way our congregation is organized," observed a member from St. Matthew's Lutheran Church. Our parish is now organized around the management-by-objective concept. We don't have the traditional functional or standing committees. Instead we have a series of task forces, many of them functioning only for a very brief period of time, and each one is charged with the responsibility for achieving certain operational goals."

"I guess we have the simplest organization of any church represented here," commented a young woman from the Green Valley Church. "Our four-hundred-member congregation is divided into twenty-five growth groups with twelve to twenty persons in each group. We meet together for worship every Sunday morning as a congregation, and occasionally there will be a meeting of representatives from the growth groups to coordinate calendar or handle some business matter, but that's very minor."

These comments illustrate several of the basic considerations which influence how a congregation is organized to carry out its responsibilities. Most Protestant congregations are organized around one of six basic models, each of which is illustrated by one or more of these congregations. These six basic models are (1) participation (illustrated by the First Christian Church and to a lesser degree by the United Methodist congregation), (2) representation (illustrated by the long-range planning committee at St. John's United Church of Christ), (3) performance (illustrated by both Westminster Presbyterian and St. Paul's Episcopal churches, with the emphasis in both cases on responsible representative church government), (4) task or mission (illustrated in different ways by both First Baptist and St. Matthew's churches), (5) seniority (illustrated by Trinity Church), and (6) satisfactions and growth (illustrated by the Green Valley Church and, to a limited degree, by St. Matthew's Lutheran Church).

There is another model which is widely used and which cuts across several of these models. This is the "consensus model." It is not listed as a separate model here, because it overlaps several of the other six, and because it is really a *style* of decision-making rather than a *model*. It is most common among Quakers, but is also widely followed in many rural congregations and in many congregations, both urban and rural, in which the decision-making process is dominated by two or three families.

It may be helpful to distinguish further between these six basic models of congregational structure.

Perhaps the most widely promoted approach to the organization of the congregation in the post–World War II era is the participation model. This maximizes the number of members who serve on boards and committees. It is based on the assumption that "the involved member is an active member, and the active member is an involved member."

Congregations using this model tend to have large governing boards with between twenty-five and two hundred members and many standing committees. A major guideline for the nominating committee is to maximize the number of members serving on boards and committees. This model is reinforced by the goal of "Let's spread the work load among more people."

The Christian Church (Disciples of Christ), the Baptists, and the Methodists have traditionally been strong proponents of the participation model, although the United Methodist Church has swung sharply toward the representation model in recent years.

In the last few years there has been a growing emphasis on the principle of representation in the organization of congregations and denominational and interdenominational agencies. Among the highly visible examples of this are the "quotas" for women, youth, and members of minority groups, the efforts to include proponents of conflicting points of view, and the inclusion of individuals by virtue of the office they hold.

In many congregations with more than five hundred confirmed members, and especially those with more than a thousand members, there is a strong emphasis on use of a performance model. In simple terms, this is building an organizational structure which facilitates "getting something done." A common example of this is the "cabinet" or "executive committee" or "steering committee" consisting of the pastor and five to ten lay persons which meets two or three times as frequently as the larger governing body (board, session, council, etc.) and is chosen with the expectation that this small group will be the key decison-making body in the congregation.

Another widespread example of the use of the performance model approach is the replacement of standing committees with task forces and ad hoc groups which are dissolved when they have completed the task for which they were originally created.

The Lutheran church council, the Episcopal vestry, and the Presbyterian session are often examples of the performance model in local church organization.

The churches' increasing emphasis on goals and the use of management by objective has increased interest in the task-oriented type of organization. To a limited degree this is reflected in the organizational structure recommended to congregations in 1968 in The United Methodist Church, although the structure for congregational self-government in Methodism is based more on the representation model than on the task model. The task model is oriented more toward ministry and less toward administration.

The seniority model is the most widely used "unofficial" model of congregational organization to be found in American Protestantism. Its use is being curtailed by limited-tenure-in-office rules, by requirements that a specified percentage of the persons named by the nominating committee must be recent new members, and by institutional survival pressures in many long-established congregations.

The smallest but probably the fastest growing model for organization of a congregation is based on the goal that every member of every board or committee should find this to be a satisfying, enjoyable, and rewarding experience. This is given a much higher priority than any of the three principles mentioned earlier.

Churches using this principle often combine a "self-nomination" process, in contrast to use of a nominating committee (for an elaboration of self-nomination see the next section in this chapter), with the use of task forces and other ad hoc groups. This both recognizes and reinforces the voluntary nature of participation by people in the life of the worshiping congregation.

In each of these six models a "trade-off" has been made as the organizational structure was developed. In each one of these six different models, in order to reinforce certain highly regarded advantages and values the congregation was willing to accept some disadvantages or limitations and to trade away other advantages and disadvantages. For example, both Episcopal and Presbyterian churches traded away the advantages—and the disadvantages—which go with widespread participation in order to reinforce the values of performance, order, and responsible representative government. The Green Valley Church traded away certain advantages which go with a more closely knit and centralized system of congregational organization in order to maximize the values of the growth groups.

The participation model with the large board tends to have difficulty making hard decisions. It may have problems of continuity because many members attend only occasionally and part of each meeting is spent playing "catch-up." Some of the regular attenders often go home frustrated, feeling, "It took three hours to transact forty minutes of business." On the plus side this model does help people become involved and it does reduce internal communication problems.

The representation model is very useful for pulpit committees, long-range planning committees, and groups which are asked to study and make recommendations on an issue or question. In each case the filing of a minority or dissenting report may help to clarify the issue for those who must make the final decision. The representation model is usually very unsatisfactory for the performance-oriented member or the person who prefers action and decisions to prolonged discussions.

The performance model is rarely compatible with the desire for a broad base of participation or for representation from all the various groups in the congregation. The larger the congregation, the greater the degree of this incompatibility.

The model which places the highest priority on the personal satisfactions of the participants will often help enlarge the base of participation, but it may complicate the setting of congregational priorities and result in a low level of performance in certain program areas. In other words, each model has both advantages and disadvantages. There is no perfect model of congregational structure or organization which maximizes all values. The important questions, however, are (1) what are the values and priorities you are seeking to maximize in your congregation, and (2) does the organizational structure used in your congregation tend to reinforce and maximize these values and priorities?

How Do You Nominate?

The procedures used for nominating people for leadership roles also influence creativity, participation, enthusiasm, and loyalty in the congregation. This can be illustrated by looking at four different nominating procedures.

The oldest approach to nominating people for official positions of influence is illustrated by the self-perpetuating board. The members of the governing board of the organization nominate the successors for the members leaving the board because of retirement, resignation, death, or disability. This process is still widely used in quasi-public agencies, by colleges, universities, and theological seminaries, in special governmental districts (sewer districts, library boards, etc.), in many different types of voluntary organizations, and in a large proportion of profit-motivated corporations. It is also used in many ecclesiastical agencies.

A common modification of this in church government is for the members of a functional committee, such as the Christian education commission, to decide among themselves who is willing to serve for another term and to "recommend" or "suggest" to the nominating committee the names of desirable candidates for the vacancies.

One of the major advantages of this procedure is that it tends to produce a board or committee of persons who will be compatible with one another and will enjoy working

29

together. It tends to increase the personal satisfactions for the members serving on that board or committee, and it greatly reduces the possibilities of conflict.

The obvious disadvantages are that the procedure tends to limit membership to persons who are personally known to members of the board and to bring together like-minded individuals. This means that it tends to bar from influential leadership roles recent new members in the organization, persons who are discontented with the present value system, goals, and operation of the board, and individuals who are not "like us." The self-perpetuating board often produces a "trade-off" of creativity, innovation, and intentional change in favor of compatibility in interpersonal relations. The limitations of this system of nominating individuals for leadership roles have been largely responsible for the demand for "independent" nominating committees.

The limitations of the self-perpetuating board have led to widespread use of what has become the most familiar process in church circles for selecting the persons to fill positions of leadership and influence. Typically, several individuals are chosen to constitute a committee which recommends to the congregation the individuals who should be elected by the members for each office and committee. Occasionally a committee will nominate two individuals for each vacancy in order to give the congregation a real choice, but usually the nominating committee is satisfied if they can find one person who will consent to be nominated for each vacancy.

In simple, nonpejorative terms this process assigns the responsibility for the allocation of the time, talent, and energy of the members to an elite group which makes the basic decisions on behalf of the total group. Usually the report of the nominating committee is adopted without open dissent, but only rarely does the act of approval produce waves of enthusiasm or encourage massive outbursts of creativity.

The popularity of this traditional procedure is diminishing with the decrease in the number of people who appreciate having an elitist group make decisions on their behalf. One of the casualties of the growing interest in participatory democracy is this traditional nominating procedure, but the replacement process is very slow.

A third procedure for nominating persons is sometimes referred to as the "football draft." Perhaps the best method of describing it is to relate what happens when it is used.

St. Andrew's is a ninety-year-old, eight-hundred-member congregation which receives an average of seventy new members annually and loses about the same number through transfers and deaths. Only the pastor, who is in his seventeenth year at St. Andrew's, knows every member by name. Three years ago several leaders became concerned about the lack of a sense of unity, the gradually narrowing base of participation in the life and ministry of the congregation, the increasing difficulty in recruiting volunteers for leadership positions and committee assignments, the impact of inflation on a slowly rising level of giving, and the general lack of enthusiasm. Out of this came the diagnosis that one of the causes of these symptoms was an excessive emphasis on keeping the institutional machinery operating and an inadequate emphasis on ministry and mission.

This diagnosis produced a decision to simplify the organizational structure of the congregation. The new structure called for the formation of twelve standing committees including worship, Christian education, membership care, evangelism, home missions, world missions, finance, trustees, the women's fellowship, the men's brotherhood, the youth council, and pastoral relations. It was decided that the church council would consist of the chairperson from these twelve organizations plus the pastor and the church treasurer. Partly in rebellion against the term "chairperson" and partly to help communicate the new organizational style more clearly, the term "coach" was used to identify the person who had the key leadership responsibility for each of the twelve committees. The twelve coaches were elected at the annual congregational meeting in January to serve

31

for the "program year" running from July 1 through June 30.

The distinctive element of this structure is the "football draft" held in late April, at which time each "coach" drafts the members for his "team." There is no limit on the numbers for each team. That decision is left to the coach.

On a Saturday afternoon in late April the twelve coaches and the pastor gather in the fellowship hall at St. Andrew's where a complete roster of the members of the congregation is displayed on one wall. Four weeks earlier, by drawing straws, the order for drafting was determined. This year the coach of the world missions team draws the longest straw and thus receives the right to draft first in each round, followed by the coach of the finance team and the coach of the women's auxiliary. The determination of the order of selection in the draft is the lead story in the week's issue of the St. Andrew's newsletter. Rumors begin to circulate on who will be the number one draft choice this year. A week before the draft the coach of the Christian education team, who drew the right to make the tenth selection in each round of the draft, announces in the church newsletter that he has traded his first-, second-, and third-round rights to the coach of the women's auxiliary for her right to choose third in the first round of the draft. This gives her the tenth rather than the third choice in the first round, but she has both the third and the tenth choices in the second and third rounds. It is obvious to everyone that he has someone in mind whom he feels he must have as a key member of his Christian education team. Who is that person who is worth three high draft choices? By the day the actual draft rolls around each coach has talked with his or her favorite prospect and found out which ones will "sign up" with that team if drafted. The rules stipulate that no member may play for more than one team. This is done to encourage broader participation, to strengthen team loyalties, to avoid over-working "the loyal core," to encourage recruitment of new and relatively unknown members, and to avoid conflicts in scheduling meeting dates. Anyone not drafted and any-

32

one who unites with St. Andrew's after the Saturday draft is a "free agent" and may be signed by any team at any time during the year. The use of the draft concept encourages use of the contract concept, in which the coach is expected to spell out to each prospective member of the team what will be expected of that person if he or she agrees to sign. Several of the teams at St. Andrew's use a written contract which spells out meeting dates and other responsibilities of the players on the particular team. Every draftee and free agent is expected to sign the contract as part of the agreement to "play" on that team. During the year a player may ask for his or her unconditional release because of the pressure of personal or business responsibilities or in order to play for another team. While this has produced some tension and a few problems, everyone agrees it is preferable to the old system in which every committee had a couple of members who never attended any meetings or carried any part of the load and a few others who were unpredictable and undependable. If agreeable to both the coach and the "player," a person may sign a two-year contract to play on the same team, but no one may play on the same one for more than four *consecutive* years.

Back when St. Andrew's used the traditional nominating committee process for selecting people for leadership roles, the pastor was the key person in the process. Since he was the only person on the nominating committee who knew every member, he tended, without meaning to do so, to dominate the nominating process. Often the pastor was the person who talked with potential nominees to discover if they would be willing to serve. This tended to increase the dominance of his role on the nominating committee. Since the football draft was inaugurated he has a far more passive and less dominant role in the selection of persons for leadership positions. The coaches, who are selected in January and may serve for a maximum of three years as coach of any one team, have at least three months to scout for potential recruits. Those who are in their second or third year as

33

coach of the same team, of course, have much longer to look for and to interview potential future draft choices. The system has shifted the initiative for identifying and recruiting leaders from one minister to twelve laypersons. The pastor plays his key role on draft Saturday. He simply sits, watches, and answers questions. For example, after about the sixth round of the draft the coach of one of the teams may come over to him and say, "Pastor, these are the six people I have chosen so far. We still need someone with these skills and these two people are still available. Which one would you recommend, or do you know someone else who is still available that I have overlooked?" The pastor, in effect, is a scout for each of the twelve teams.

A significant advantage of this process lies in the "free agent" concept. This means every person who joins the congregation after draft Saturday in April is a free agent and may be approached at any time during the year by a coach who feels a need to strengthen his team or to replace a player who moved away.

The most serious problem at St. Andrew's came in the third year. On the tenth round of the draft the coach of the finance committee "drafted" a close friend of his who was a member of the Presbyterian church across the street. He argued for the legitimacy of his decision by declaring, "George has been a member of that church for six years and has never been asked to serve on any committee or on the session. He told me last week that if I drafted him he would be glad to transfer his membership over here to St. Andrew's." Led by the pastor, who accused the coach of proselytizing, eight of the other coaches voted to declare this an illegal draft. The other three coaches voted in favor of "raiding the other league" and supported the coach of the finance committee. One of the three suggested the names of four inactive members of St. Andrew's who could be offered as compensation in return for the Presbyterian layman, but no one took him seriously.

A less serious problem came up when several members

appeared on draft Saturday to watch, cheer, offer unsolicited advice, heckle the coaches, suggest trades, and second-guess the process. The first reaction of three or four coaches was to urge that this be declared a closed meeting. Another longtime member broke the tension when he remarked, "Five or six years ago I was on the nominating committee here at St. Andrew's, and we never did have a meeting with 100 percent attendance. We complained about that and changed our system. Which problem do you prefer—having a process in which you can't get the members of the nominating committee to show up, or a process where we not only have every member of the nominating committee here, but also a bunch of interested spectators? I think we traded up when we traded problems!" The third year nearly 150 spectators watched the beginning of the draft. How many members come out to watch the nominating committee in your congregation?

Only in relatively few congregations today does the nominating process arouse the interest that is so visible every April at St. Andrew's. Far more important, after three years of experience the leaders at St. Andrew's report that use of the football draft style of selecting leaders has broadened the base of participation, produced an increased commitment to their responsibilities on the part of the members of the various committees, reduced apathy, encouraged creativity, increased enthusiasm, opened new doors for participation by new members, changed the role of the pastor in the leadership recruitment process to more of an advisory or consultative one, and had a clearly favorable impact on the giving level. The new system also produced programs of excessive competitiveness, to use the football analogy, and some hurt feelings on the part of members who were not drafted in the first two or three rounds or were completely ignored. In comparing these problems with the old set of problems, most of the members at St. Andrew's believe they "traded up" when they replaced the elitist nominating committee with the football draft.

A fourth procedure for nominating persons for leadership positions in the congregation is the self-nomination process.

At Forest Hill Church all the offices, tasks, and committee positions which in the typical congregation are filled by recommendation of the nominating committee are listed on two very large posters by a coordinating committee whose members nominated themselves the previous year. For each opening three vacant lines are drawn on the nominating poster. Thus for the three vacancies for the board of trustees the number three is written in to show the number of vacant positions, but there are nine lines on which members may sign up in this self-nominating process.

The green poster lists those positions which require a major investment of time and energy. These include church school teachers, members of the twelve-member governing board for Forest Hill, members of the chancel choir, the treasurer, the chairperson of all committees, the trustees, the financial secretary, and a dozen other types of positions. The yellow poster lists those jobs which will require a much smaller investment of time and energy. These include the committee to plan the July all-church picnic, the eighty-member church council, which meets quarterly to hear and act on major policy issues referred to it by the board, and many other jobs. A ceiling is placed on the number of positions for which an individual may volunteer. Each person is limited to a maximum of two major (green poster) and three minor (yellow poster) positions. If more people sign up than there are actual openings—and this is encouraged— a "runoff" election is held. (All new adult members are asked at the time they unite with the church to pick one board or committee they would like to serve on and are assigned to that board or committee even if it is "filled.")

The coordinating committee is responsible for supervising this entire process including the publicity and the elections. If (and this happens nearly every year) no one signs up for certain vacancies those positions are left vacant. The basic rule is that it is better to be a few members short on a committee or to combine Sunday school classes than to coerce unwilling people into responsibilities they would rather not have.

The first two years were difficult years at Forest Hill Church as they experimented with this procedure. Several of the longtime members and veteran leaders were sure it would not work and repeatedly tried to scrap it in favor of the old system with an elitist nominating committee. The agreement in the beginning, however, had been to give this new system a two-year trial. At the end of two years, at a remarkably well-attended congregational meeting, the vote was 113 to 47 in favor of continuing the self-nomination process. Nearly all those who spoke in opposition to the self-nomination process were longtime members in their forties and fifties who had served in leadership positions for years.

Those who spoke in favor of continuing the self-nominating process pointed to the much larger base of participation; the opportunities for creativity and growth in letting people pick their responsibilities; the great increase in participation by younger members; the fact that for the first time in the history of Forest Hill Church women were now serving on the twelve-member governing board and as trustees; the many dire predictions ("What if no one signs up to be church treasurer? Who will keep the books?") which had not materialized; and the increase in the trust level in the congregation.

Many congregations use a combination of two or three of these procedures in their nominating process. A common one is the combination of the self-perpetuating board and the talent search. In the talent search, which is a variation of self-nomination, each member is asked to fill out a form indicating the roles, tasks, or committees he or she may feel called to serve in as a member of the congregation. The information secured from this talent search is shared with the various functional committees, as well as with the nominating committee, and is used as the members of the committees suggest names to be nominated to serve on them. This increases the chances of perpetuating committees of compatible and like-minded persons, but it may not reach the shy and the bashful or the less well known new members. All these examples show how the nominating process is a very important factor in encouraging or discouraging creativity, initative, and participation.

How Do You Vote?

"I don't know what we should do next, but we can't live with that vote," declared the chairman of the music committee at North Street Church. "Why in the world do we let half of the members defeat the purchase of a new organ when the other half want it and are willing to pay for it? What kind of a church is this when one of the strongest proponents of a new organ ends up voting against it in the interests of peace and harmony?" He was discussing the fate of the committee's recommendation that the church should purchase a new organ. After several months of study the nine-member music committee had voted seven to one (with one member abstaining because she expected to move out of the community at the end of the year) to recommend replacing the old organ at a net cost of $38,000. This recommendation was forwarded to the board, which, by a twenty-nine to seventeen vote, endorsed it and urged its approval at a congregational meeting.

The debate at the specially called congregational meeting was hot, loud, and long. Finally, after three hours, a vote was taken and the recommendation to purchase the new organ was approved 188 to 186. When the vote was announced, Bill Adams, a leading attorney in town and one of the most highly respected members of the congregation, asked for reconsideration, explaining, "While I favor replacing this old clunker we call an organ and I voted to support the recommendation of the music committee, in a voluntary association such as a church, we cannot act favorably on such a costly venture without a much larger majority. Therefore I am asking for reconsideration in order to cast my vote against the proposal. I am doing this because many people may misconstrue a two-vote majority as a decision. In a voluntary association a two-vote majority on a divisive issue should be interpreted as a decision not to go ahead. Therefore I am asking for reconsideration so that I can vote against it and hopefully we can eliminate any misunderstandings before they develop."

On this second vote Bill Adams was joined by three others who had voted for a new organ earlier, and the final vote was 184 in favor of a new organ and 190 against. It was clear to nearly everyone that the proposal to replace the old organ was dead.

What happened?

On the surface it appears that the proposal to purchase a new organ at North Street Church died for lack of a substantial majority.

A more careful examination of this event reveals that the decision-making and voting process at North Street Church, and in thousands of other congregations, has been "stacked" to reward negativism, perpetuate the status quo, block change, encourage apathy, stifle initiative, provoke discontent, and cause active leaders to drop into inactivity because of discouragement, frustration, and irritation.

In simpler and more specific terms, the voting process at North Street Church counts the votes rather than weighing them and places more emphasis on counting the "no" votes than on weighing the "yes" votes.

This point can be illustrated in more positive terms by three examples.

At Maple Hill Church the trustees debated a proposal to purchase pew cushions. After consulting with the finance committee the trustees unanimously voted against the purchase of pew cushions because "the funds are not available." This decision was confirmed by the board a few weeks later,

39

and everyone agreed that the proposal had been killed, not because of lack of interest, but because of lack of money.

Several months later an elderly widowed member of Maple Hill came into the church office and asked, "When will those new cushions be installed?" The secretary gently told her that the trustees had investigated the proposal, found it would cost four thousand dollars, and concluded that it was beyond the available financial resources of the congregation at that time. A week later the widow sent in a check for four thousand dollars and asked that the money be used to install pew cushions.

What happened?

The voting process had been changed. Earlier it had been assumed that a majority vote of both the trustees and the board would be needed to approve the proposal to buy pew cushions. When they counted the votes the "no" votes outnumbered the "yes" votes and the proposal was killed. Later the voting process was changed to one in which only the "yes" votes were counted. A total of four thousand "yes" votes was required to "approve" the proposal to purchase pew cushions. The "yes" votes were a dollar apiece. When the widow cast four thousand "yes" votes the pew cushions had the necessary majority! No one bothered to count the "no" votes.

A second example is the program-planning process in the women's organization in a Nashville, Tennessee, congregation. In many congregations the special "projects" of the women's organization are chosen at a business meeting by use of the majority vote procedure. Frequently several women develop great enthusiasm for a specific proposal, and they are disappointed when their proposal fails to win the support of the majority as a long list is reduced to two or three or four approved projects. The "no" votes kill the others.

In the Nashville church, however, the women do not count the "no" votes. They count only the "yes" votes. Once a year the monthly meeting devotes about ninety minutes to "voting" on the projects. Every individual woman or group of women in the organization that has a specific action proposal or project to suggest is invited to submit it at what is described as the "county fair." This meeting is held in the fellowship hall of the church, and the space next to the walls is divided up among those who have specific projects to propose. One year along the west wall, for example, those in attendance saw a woman at a card table inviting others to sign up for her project, which was to secure commitments from four other women to make weekly visits to some of the lonely people in a nursing home. Next to her table was a booth at which three women displayed their proposal that the group raise a thousand dollars for equipment for a church school in Hong Kong. Next to that was a color slide presentation by two women who were looking for allies to help finance and staff a six-week-long day camp the following summer, which would be a shared venture for inner-city and suburban children. Next to this presentation was a display by three women who proposed that one of the projects for the coming year be buying a new carpet, reupholstering the furniture, and painting the church parlor, which had been neglected since it was refurbished in 1946. The last display along this wall was initiated by one woman who was proposing that the women's organization accept the challenge to recruit six volunteers who would go on their own time and at their own expense to help enlarge a children's hospital in Haiti. The goal was six volunteer workers and three thousand dollars for materials.

For an hour and a half the women walk around the fellowship hall visiting various booths and displays and listening to the "sales pitch" offered at each booth or display. As they walk around the hall they "vote" for their choices by signing up as volunteers for a specific project, by pledging money, and/or by committing their support for a particular program goal. Some women sign up to work on two or three or four projects, while a few make only financial pledges, and a couple find nothing that attracts their support. There are two ground rules. First, each person or group has to quantify the resources necessary to implement their proposal. This includes the number of volunteers, the amount of money required if financial resources are necessary, and any other required resources. The second ground rule is that the voting is over when the bell rings at the end of ninety minutes. Any proposal which does not secure the required support by the time the bell rings is not approved. This means, for example, that if the women promoting the day camp proposal do not find both their quota of volunteers to help staff the summer day camp *and* the necessary financial commitments by the time the bell rings, the project is not approved. It should be noted that this process completely eliminates the casting, as well as the counting, of "no" votes. The women are asked only to express their affirmative opinion. No one has to vote against any proposal.

The first year this procedure was used it produced considerable frustration. Many of the women complained that ninety minutes did not give them enough time to hear, compare, evaluate, and respond to the many different proposals. By the second year, however, all those with pet projects were out weeks before the day of the county fair, stirring up interest, hanging their ideas on the grapevine, and making trades for support ("I'll sign up for your project if you sign up for mine next year"). One of the benefits of this procedure is the subtle distinction between a proposal's being rejected and its simply not being approved. After the first year the women saw this distinction more clearly. If a particular proposal did not receive the necessary support to be approved, that did not mean it had been rejected. Many of the women brought back for the following year a proposal which had not secured the necessary support the first year it was presented. In several cases two or three women who had a "great idea" and were disappointed when an insufficient number signed up for it the first year it was presented made sure there was sufficient support when they brought it back the second year. In at least two instances the new supporters helped improve the proposal by their suggestions.

The third example of a more affirmative approach to decision-making involves a congregation which, like the North Street Church, was considering purchase of a new organ. When the recommendation to purchase a $65,000 organ came from the music committee at Bethel Church to the board, it was held for two months while three other committees finished their work. One of them recommended that Bethel Church contribute $9,000 a year for at least three years toward a cooperative ministry to "alienated street kids." This proposal called for Bethel and two other congregations to share the responsibility for this specialized ministry. A second committee recommended that Bethel Church call a third minister who would devote 85 to 90 percent of his time to a ministry to single adults beginning with one-parent families. This recommendation carried a $28,000 annual price tag. The other committee recommended a three-year, $90,000 program to acquire the three old houses immediately south of the Bethel property, raze them, and utilize the cleared land for a combination neighborhood playground and offstreet parking facility.

These four recommendations were combined into one presentation to the thirteen hundred members of Bethel Church. Instead of asking for a definitive vote at a congregational meeting, however, the board used a different "voting" procedure. The presentation to the members did not ask for a traditional ballot. Instead the board announced that it was commending all four proposals to the members. Approval would be dependent on the members' response. If and when $65,000 is pledged to the organ fund, the music committee will be auhorized to go ahead with the purchase and installation of a new organ. If and when $9,000 is pledged to the cooperative ministry to alienated street youth, the Bethel representatives on the joint committee will be authorized to commit Bethel Church to this cooperative ministry. If and when $28,000 is pledged to the pro-

43

posed ministry to single adults, the committee which proposed this will be authorized to begin the search for a minister to staff it. If and when $90,000 is pledged to the playground–parking lot proposal, the property committee will be authorized to proceed with the acquisition, clearance, and redevelopment of the land south of the church building. Members can vote for as many or as few of these four proposals as they wish, and they may vote as often as they desire. Votes are one dollar apiece. No one is forced to oppose any of the four recommendations. The members who consider a new organ to be an unnecessary luxury are not structured into a position where they have no choice but to oppose it. They can ignore it and concentrate their time, energy, enthusiasm, and money on what they favor. It is clearly understood that these four recommendations are to be financed by "second-mile giving" and by designated funds from bequests, legacies, and memorials.

The common distinctive characteristic of the decision-making process used in each of these three churches is that they do not count the "no" votes. Instead the decision-making process has been restructured to accentuate the affirmative and to be supportive of diversity and pluralism. In each of these three congregations it has been necessary to help the members see that the unity of the congregation lies in Christ, not in conformity. In each of these three congregations the decision-making process has been shifted from the traditional choosing of sides in a "for" and "against" battle to a structure which encourages each person to identify what he is "for" without feeling constrained to oppose those ideas and programs which do not attract his interest.

Manipulation in Church Finances

Another area where the structural organization of the congregation influences values, attitudes, and priorities is in church finances. This can be illustrated by showing the expenditure budget of the average congregation to an average member and asking the open-ended question "Before we talk about your commitment to Jesus Christ and how much of your tithe you want to allocate to helping finance the ministry and mission of this congregation,[2] do you have any questions or comments about this proposed budget for our church for the coming year?"

As this average member looks over the sheet of paper which shows the proposed expenditures for salaries, pensions, office expenses, building maintenance, mortgage payments, insurance, utilities, benevolences, and other items, he will probably respond with questions or comments such as these: "Why is our insurance up nearly a fourth over last year?" "Golly, you folks certainly have done a remarkable job in holding the increase to only 2 percent when the price of everything else is going up!" "I never realized that we had to spend that much just on utilities! Isn't there any way that can be cut down?" "It seems to me that a lot of the material for the Sunday school could be saved and used again next year. That way we could reduce that big item for church school supplies." "I don't know how you can expect me to increase my pledge when the preacher makes more than I do and gets a free house and utilities besides."

The responses tend to be radically different when the same average member is asked the same question, but instead of being handed a copy of the typical expenditures budget he is given a sheet which summarizes the proposed budget in this form:

---

[2] Those who assume that every tither gives the entire tithe to the church of which he or she is a member may have some difficulty with the phrasing of this question. The phrasing used here is based on the assumption that a growing proportion of church members who tithe allocate only a fraction of that tithe to the congregation to which they belong and allocate the balance to a variety of other religious, charitable, educational, and philanthropic causes. This is a trend which is encouraged by many regional judicatories when they "authorize" church-related homes, hospitals, colleges, and seminaries to contact church members for direct gifts.

45

Ministry to the members of this congregation 85%
Ministry to this community beyond
    the membership   9%
Ministry beyond this community   6%
Total   100%

When this is identified as a summary of the proposed expenditure budget for the coming year, the average member will usually respond with comments or questions such as these: "I never realized we spend such a large proportion of the budget on ourselves!" "Do you mean to tell me that eighty-five cents out of every dollar in our budget is spent on ourselves?" "It seems to me that 6 percent for ministry beyond this community isn't very much." "I'm glad to see we're spending more on mission here than we're sending away, but I would like to see that 9 percent increased to maybe 12 or 15 percent for ministry here in this community."

Why the differences between these two sets of responses?

The basic reason for these differences lies in the manner in which the material is presented. In the first example the initial presentation influenced the members to think in terms of money and costs. When a normal human being is presented with information which causes him to think of money and costs, the natural response is frequently "That's too much!" This tendency is illustrated by the person who inquires how much he will have to pay if he trades his old automobile in for a new model, by the individual in the checkout line at the supermarket when the cashier adds up the cost of two bags of groceries, by the father who asks how much that new dress for his daughter cost, by parents when they buy new shoes for all three children on the same day, and by the church member who is handed a sheet detailing the church's proposed expenditures for the coming year. In each of these illustrations the emphasis on money and costs produces an immediate negative response. This tendency toward a negative response whenever costs are introduced is greatly enhanced during an inflationary era.

In the second example the initial presentation of the church budget is developed around the theme of ministry. The basic categories are not dollar expenditure items, but rather areas of ministry. The format of the presentation causes the member to think in terms of proportions and to compare the expenditures for ministry to the membership with the expenditures for ministry to others. This tends to produce a more affirmative, although often critical, response.

In both examples the method or format used influences behavior patterns. This is not the point, since there are no "neutral" approaches. The point is that one approach tends to influence the recipient of the information to respond negatively and the other tends to influence the person receiving the information to think in terms of the definition of purpose, role, and nature of the Christian church. Both are "manipulative" in that both influence people's responses. Which represents creative church administration? Which represents a counterproductive approach to church administration? Which one subverts the efforts to help each develop his "frame of reference" about the church around ministry rather than money?

Self-Defeating Behavior

Psychologists, sociologists, psychiatrists, and counselors have defined what is often referred to as a "self-defeating pattern of behavior." Occasionally this can be seen in churches, when an action which is taken to achieve a specific goal is carried out in a manner which in fact tends to reduce the chances of achieving that goal. The format used in presenting the church budget may be creative or it may be self-defeating. There are many other examples of self-defeating behavior which are so widely practiced that they merit the attention of anyone interested in the subject of creative church administration.

One of these will be familiar to most readers. It concerns the assimilation of husbands into the life and fellowship of the worshiping congregation. Four patterns in the churches can be observed repeatedly. The first is that the new members who tend to be assimilated into the life, ministry, and fellowship of the congregation are those who very quickly identify with a group (choir, Sunday school class, circle, study group, work area, committee, etc.) and/or who move into a role (teacher, officer, leader, etc.) which helps them identify with the congregation they have just joined. The second is that in most congregations there are more groups and roles for women than for men. The third pattern is that not infrequently six months after a new couple in the community join the church she is an active member and he is relatively inactive. The fourth pattern is reflected in the frequently heard comment "If it weren't for the willingness of the women to carry more than their share of the load this congregation would be in bad shape!" Occasionally someone will explain the involvement of the wife and the inactivity of the husband by noting that "everyone knows women tend to be more religious than men." Few point out that the assimilation process in most churches tends to keep husbands from becoming assimilated into the life of the fellowship.

Closely related is another form of self-defeating behavior, which can often be identified by the comment "We decided to leave the restaurant business to private enterprise, and so the kitchen in our church is almost never used."

In every culture the act of eating together provides an important opportunity for meaningful fellowship. The Last Supper is one illustration. Other examples are the business luncheon, the family meal, the banquet for a special occasion, and the picnic.

The congregation which closes the church kitchen must replace these occasions for fellowship with other equally

48

meaningful events or it will be without several of the most useful methods for assimilating newcomers, for helping people become better acquainted, and for facilitating many other aspects of ministry to people. In too many congregations the elimination of the all-church picnic, the carry-in or covered-dish dinner, and the potluck supper has been a self-defeating action.

A third form of self-defeating behavior can be found in many of those congregations which periodically send out to each member or each household a statement of financial contributions to date. This is usually done as a reminder, to provide a record for the member's own benefit, as a means of helping each member keep up-to-date on the annual financial pledge, and also to raise money.

In the churches which send this statement out immediately following the last Sunday of the month the largest offering is usually the one received on the first Sunday of the month.

In other congregations, however, these statements are mailed twice a year, once in July and once in January. By waiting until January to send out the final statement these churches are able to reduce the impact of this statement on actual giving since it is received (a) after the end of the giving period, (b) after the end of the tax year for most individuals, and (c) after the books are presumed to be closed on the church's fiscal year. By waiting until after the first of the new year to send out these financial statements the church is suggesting, "We are sorry you did not contribute as much as you pledged, but it is too late now since the church year has ended for us and the end of the tax year has passed for you. Hopefully you will do better next year." (In 1978, 1979, and 1980 December will have five Sundays. Thus the churches wanting to avoid this pattern of self-defeating behavior can send the "year-to-date" statement immediately following the fourth Sunday in December and the annual statement for income tax purposes in January.)

Closely related to this is the form or appearance of the statement which is sent out to members reporting the record

49

of their giving to date. Who is the "client" for this form or statement? The financial secretary or church bookkeeper? Or the person who will receive the statement? Judging by their appearance most of these forms seem to have been designed by bookkeepers for the convenience of other bookkeepers. The result is that all too often receiving one of these statements in the mail arouses a response in the church member similar to that provoked by a bill from a department store or a notice that one's income tax report has been audited and one owes $371 in back taxes and penalties.

A much more productive approach is to prepare two or three versions of a brief form letter, in each of which there are blank spaces in which the financial secretary can write in the amount of the pledge and the amount received to date from the recipient of the letter. One version of his form letter would be directed toward those persons who made a financial pledge to the church and are up-to-date or ahead on their contributions. A second version can be directed to those members who did not pledge, but are making regular contributions of record. The third version can be directed to those who pledged, but are behind schedule in meeting their commitment.

An even more attractive approach is used in a Florida congregation where an amateur cartoonist prepares a six-panel cartoon to replace the quarterly statement. The characters in the cartoon discuss the state of the church's financial health and in two of the "balloons" carrying this conversation blank spaces are left for the financial secretary to write in the amount pledged and the amount received from the recipient of that particular sheet of paper. A new cartoon is prepared each quarter to reflect the reality of that point in the history of the church's finances.

Another widespread example of self-defeating behavior is the opposition to the formation of meaningful fellowship groups within the congregation. Frequently this opposition is expressed in a statement such as "We don't want any of the groups in this church turning into cliques, so we insist that no one be permitted to remain in the same group for more than one year." [3]

Most serious efforts to build strong, tightly knit supportive groups in which membership is especially meaningful to the members face this "trade-off" question. The trade-off is usually the trading off of turnover and ease of entry for newcomers in favor of continuity, cohesiveness, loyalty, and mutual support. The required annual (or quarterly) turnover of membership usually produces receptivity to newcomers, erratic attendance, limited loyalty to the group, and a lack of cohesiveness.

A sixth form of self-defeating behavior is found in the ✳ evaluation processes of many congregations. A very common example of it is represented by this brief conversation:

"We really worked hard on this, and I believe this will be one of the most meaningful special worship services for our people that we have had here in a long time."

"I'm terribly disappointed! After all that work we only had half as many people here as we expected."

These two comments about the same event suggest that the focus in the first was on quality but that the "evaluation" reflected in the second was based on quantity.

Increasingly the emphasis in the churches is on quality and on programs, events, and ministries which will be meaningful to people. When it is over, instead of focusing the evaluation on what happened, the self-defeating pattern is to ask, "How many were there?"

After decades of training church people to evaluate by the attendance record, it is very difficult to change the focus for evaluation to quality.

Closely related is the form of self-defeating behavior sum-✳

---

[3] To understand this point it is essential that the reader understand the difference between a "group" and a "clique." The group to which *I* belong is a very meaningful mutual support group committed to the personal and spiritual growth of the members and to reflecting Christ's love for us by our ministry to our neighbor. The group to which *you* belong is a clique trying to run this church!

marized in the edict "There will be no money-making activities of any kind in this congregation. This church will be supported entirely by the tithes and offerings of the members!"

~ To understand this issue it is necessary to make three introductory distinctions. First, there is a vast difference between the method of financing the life, program, and ministry of a worshiping congregation and the sponsorship by a congregation of "money-making" events. In many congregations all dollar expenditures, including building programs and benevolences, come from the contributions of the members in the offering plate. The receipts from the money-making activities held once or twice a year are given away. It is not unusual to find congregations with a standing rule that the receipts from all money-making activities must be used for benevolent and charitable purposes or simply "must be given away." In churchy terms, the receipts from the money-making events become second-mile giving.

~ The second important distinction is in how people express themselves. Some people feel very competent and comfortable expressing themselves, their commitment to Jesus Christ as Lord and Savior, and their attachment to the congregation of which they are a member, through verbal skills. Many others feel much more comfortable expressing themselves through creative skills, by making things.[4] As many congregations drift in the direction of placing a premium on verbal skills, they tend to eliminate the opportunities for expression by use of creative skills. Dropping the annual bazaar, the July strawberry social, and the October church dinner has deprived many church members of the chance to express themselves.

~ The third distinction is between being received as a new adult member into the membership of the congregation and being received into the fellowship of that church. For many new adult members entrance into the fellowship circle came

[4] For an elaboration of this point see Lyle E. Schaller, *Hey, That's Our Church!* (Nashville: Abingdon Press, 1975), pp. 141-42.

through their participation in money-making activities.

One form of institutionally self-defeating behavior is the elimination of the fellowship events which encourage the use of creative skills without replacing them with other methods of assimilating newcomers into the fellowship circle, and without making other meaningful opportunities for people to express themselves through their creativity!

Another form of self-defeating behavior has been identified earlier in this chapter and, in a sense, is the theme of this entire book. Do our organizational structures, our processes for selecting leaders, and our decision-making processes tend to thwart our purposes and goals as a congregation? Perhaps the easiest way to illustrate this and to sum up this chapter is to be somewhat redundant.

It is the practice of many congregations to ask the members to vote on proposals for change. The proposal may be to shift from one to two worship services on Sunday morning, or to relocate the meeting place, or to undertake a special program of outreach, or to share a pastor with another congregation, or to change the age of confirmation for children, or to adopt a new liturgy.

Too often this is presented in a form which asks people to vote "yes" or "no" on the proposed change. This procedure has several counterproductive features. Many people naturally oppose any change the first time it is suggested, and thus there is a built-in bias toward a negative vote. A "yes-no" vote tends to be divisive since it produces both "winners" and "losers." Too often a negative vote is accepted as final when it should be interpreted only as a preliminary response. If the majority vote "No," this may be instructive on what not to do, but it is not necessarily very helpful in deciding what should be done.

A better approach, when obliged to seek a "vote" on a question, is to phrase the alternatives as *(a)* yes, let's do that or *(b)* yes, let's do this (which may be a continuation of the status quo), with the probable consequences identified.

The best approach in many situations is to avoid a vote until a consensus has emerged.

It is only one short step from this discussion of self-defeating behavior to the subject of "planning models," for in the selection of the planning model they will use many congregations condemn themselves to another form of self-defeating behavior and thus thwart what otherwise could be creative and productive efforts to plan for ministry.

Planning Models

"It should be perfectly obvious to everyone that the number one priority here should be youth and young married couples," declared a longtime leader at Ebenezer Church. "The future of the church is with the young people! Jim and I went over the membership roll last night in preparation for this meeting, and out of our 243 resident members, 209 are at least forty years old. Nearly half of those are past fifty-five! We do not have anyone in a leadership position under forty. We have only 14 members in the twenty to thirty age group, and 9 of them are really inactive. I don't see how anyone can look at those figures and come out with any other conclusion. We need to put more emphasis on our ministry to youth!"

"You're right, Martha," agreed another older leader. "We do a pretty good job here at Ebenezer for couples in their fifties and sixties, but there is no future for our church in that age group. There's no question but that reaching out to young couples should be our top priority."

"I couldn't agree with you both more," added a man who was generally recognized to be the most influential leader at Ebenezer Church. "I know it's easy to list a lot of other problems we have here. The Sunday school is down to a handful of kids, we're hurting financially, we need more parking, and we're short of leaders; but those are really symptoms of a more basic problem. If two dozen young adults joined the congregation next Sunday, all of these other problems would soon disappear!"

This approach to planning, priority-setting, and decision-making is not unusual. It is one of the most widely used "planning models" to be found in the churches. For the purposes of this discussion it can be identified as "planning from weakness." Or, to be more specific, this planning model appears to be based on the assumption that the best approach to planning is to identify that area of ministry in which our church is least effective or that function of the church in which we as a congregation are weakest and make it the number one priority. This means concentrating on that specialized area of ministry in which the resources are the fewest, past experiences will be least effective, and local skills are the scarcest. There may be other approaches which have a greater probability of failure than this planning-from-weakness model, but it is very difficult to name more than two or three. There may be other techniques which are more likely to undermine the morale of a congregation, but they are very rare. There may be other administrative processes which are more likely to be nonproductive, but they too are fortunately very rare.

Planning from Strength

A far better planning model for use a Ebenezer Church would be one which can be identified as "planning from strength" or the "potentialities model."

Recently the leaders in a congregation very similar to Ebenezer Church began asking themselves, "Where do we go from here?" As they sought to respond to this question they first concluded that they must do so within the context of the call to be faithful and obedient, rather than from a concern to perpetuate the institution. Next they asked two questions. First, what are the needs of people to which we can address ourselves as servants of Jesus Christ? Second, what are the special gifts, resources, strengths, talents, and assets we are blessed with that suggest a direction? As they reflected on the eighty years of the congregation's life, they began to realize that in the three decades since the end of World War II they had changed from a two-generation "family church" to a congregation of one-generation households, most which had already seen the youngest child leave home. They had become a congregation in which 83 of the 191 names on the mailing list represented one-person households. Instead of planning from weakness in an attempt to re-create yesterday, they saw themselves with a meeting place in a neighborhood with an increasing proportion of older residents. Many of these individuals, a large number of whom were widowed, had no active affiliation with any worshiping congregation. As they studied this picture the leaders saw the needs and the hurts of scores of lonely older persons. They also saw that this coincided with the greatest strength of their own congregation—the ability to minister to older persons, to be a family for those who had no family, to be a support group for the bereaved, and to bring the gospel of Good News to those who felt there no longer was any good news.

Within the space of fourteen months this congregation created a Bible study–prayer group–quilting fellowship of eleven older women, most of them widowed, who met all day every Tuesday and Thursday. Another group of older persons came together every Friday morning for Bible study, fellowship, and lunch and spent the afternoon calling on residents of four nearby nursing homes. A third group was formed around the idea of a "Fisherman's Club." Following a carry-in supper and a thirty-five-minute Bible study period they went out by twos in a visitation-evangelism program based on the assumption that a minimum of seven calls was necessary on any unchurched person before they could tell whether or not that individual might be interested in uniting with their congregation. A fourth group was formed to call regularly on the growing number of shut-ins in the congregation. A fifth group met every Tuesday evening for intercessory prayer. A sixth group was composed of nine men, four of them widowed, who met at the church every other Saturday to spend the day going out into the neighborhood to put up storm windows, repair front steps, fix leaky faucets, and perform a hundred other "handyman" chores for residents who could not do these things for themselves and did not feel they could afford to hire someone to do it. Every noon two or three of the wives of men in this group served a hearty lunch at the church for the corps of "neighborhood volunteers."

Twenty-six months after the first meeting of the planning committee which led to the development of the groups a statistical summary revealed that seventy-eight persons—fifty-five of them widowed, divorced, separated, or never married—were involved regularly in the life of these six groups. All but three of the seventy-eight had passed their fifty-fifth birthday, and thirty-seven of the seventy-eight were new members of the congregation. Another 119 persons, again all but three age fifty-five or over, had united with the congregation as a result of the intensive visitation-evangelism program.

When this statistical summary was being discussed by the leaders of another, similar congregation, someone asked, "But what's the future of a congregation which specializes in a ministry to older persons?"

One response was "That's an irrelevant question; the point is, are they being faithful and obedient in responding to what the Lord is calling them to do and to be?"

A more pragmatic-minded person responded, "They have a great future! They're specializing in a ministry to the most neglected and the second-fastest-growing age group in the total population."

Planning by Cliché

A third planning model in wide use across the North American continent today can be identified simply as "planning by cliché." All too often simplistic clichés, which later turn out to be fallacies, are offered as the solution to the problems facing the church.

Unquestionably the most common of these clichés is "Ours ✱ is a friendly church, and that's our main attraction for people."

While it is true that in most congregations many of the recent new members commend the friendliness of the congregation, this is counting only some of the ballots. Rare is the church which counts the number of persons who visited once or twice and never came back. Though friendliness is a wonderful attribute, it is not a substitute in the long run for opportunities for personal and spiritual growth nor for excellence in program, especially in preaching and music. Likewise the number of different opportunities for people to be actively involved in ministry is far more significant than the number of "friendly" people. Every congregation has lots of "friendly" people in it. Every open, friendly, extroverted, and gregarious person finds friendly people wherever he goes. How "friendly" is the friendly church to the lonely, the alienated, the shy, the introverted, and the overburdened? That's another question!

While this dependence on "friendliness" represents the most extreme example of planning by cliché, it does not stand alone. There are at least five other examples of this planning model which deserve review here.

"If only we can reach the youth and keep them, that'll ✱ be our church of tomorrow."

Many churches launch a youth ministry in order to strengthen "our church tomorrow." This pattern has four built-in areas of self-deception. First, that is a very poor motive for developing a ministry to youth. Second, only rarely in a vigorous and growing *urban* congregation will more than 10 or 15 percent of the high school youth of 1956 be members in 1976. They move away or join another church. Third, almost invariably the urban congregation in which more than 30 percent of today's adult leaders are people who were reared in that congregation is a church in trouble. Usually the source of the problem is that the congregation has been unable to reach new people and assimilate them into leadership positions, and thus it has been forced to depend heavily for leadership on persons who are children or spouses of members. Fourth, all too frequently this cliché can be translated into operational English as "Let's place a top priority on a ministry to youth, as the youth will grow up to share our values and be like us." The problem here is the tremendous shortage of high school youth in the 1970's who want to grow up to be "like us"!

The apartment boom of the past two decades has produced a third cliché for this list: "When the apartment buildings proposed for this area are constructed, there will be hundreds of people living within walking distance of our church; and many will come here and become members of this congregation."

Though this is not heard as often as it was a decade ago, before the failure of most congregations to reach the lonely people in apartments became so widely publicized, it is still a frequently encountered cliché. The general rule on this subject is that the congregations which are reaching an increasing number of people will reach apartment dwellers, and the churches which were not reaching many new people before the apartments were constructed will not reach the new apartment residents. Apartment dwellers, like other adults, tend to participate in the life of those congregations where they have friends and/or relatives among the members. Since most residents of new apartment structures have neither friends nor relatives in the congregations which meet in nearby buildings, one of two things happens. Either the apartment dwellers stay away from the nearby congregations, or members of these congregations seek out the apartment residents and take the initiative in building friendship ties.

A fourth cliché that is encountered frequently can be summarized in this statement: "If we could just unite these

60

two or three churches here, we could create one larger congregation which could do more in ministry."

This cliché can be heard most frequently in those fifteen hundred counties which have experienced a decline in population since 1950 and in many parts of the larger central cities. In both cases experience suggests that the arithmetic comes out two plus two equals three (and often two) or three plus three plus three equals four or five. Mergers usually produce a decrease in the number of people in contact with that place where the Word is preached and the sacraments are duly administered. The merger of a large congregation and a small one tends to produce a situation which can be described more realistically as absorption rather than union.

Closely related is a fifth cliché which is often expressed in these words: "If we're ever going to reach more people, ✳ we have to move to a new location." This statement is heard most frequently in hundreds of central-city congregations with a declining membership figure.

While many relocations have produced larger and stronger congregations, especially those that were carried out before 1965, this does not automatically happen in every case. In a majority of relocations studied that were carried out during the past ten years, it appears that the two critical variables were (1) the larger the membership of the relocating congregation, the more likely it was that the church was unable to reach residents of the community in which the new meeting place was constructed, and (2) the relocated congregations which tended to grow in membership at a new location were the congregations which were growing in size before relocation.

In general, the congregations most likely to grow in membership following relocation are those which before relocation is proposed have developed the capability of reaching and assimilating unchurched persons, rather than those which relocate in order to perpetuate an institutional name and a congregation of people.

The last in this set of examples of planning by cliché is developed more adequately in chapter 10, but it should be mentioned here because it is heard so frequently.

✻ "If we can bring in programs and ministries so the building is used every day of the week, that will attract people, and our membership will increase."

Occasionally this does happen. New members are attracted by what the church is doing in ministry. Rarely, however, do many of the people toward whom the program is directed (such as the parents of children in a day care center or senior citizens) join the congregation housing the program. A far more typical pattern is that the congregation redefines its purpose as acting in a landlord role and the membership continues to decline in numbers.

The new members who do join those congregations with a heavily used building seven days a week tend overwhelmingly to be attraced, not by the programs themselves, but by an activist style of ministry, by the servant role definition of purpose (which is far different from the landlord role), and by the opportunity to serve (rather than to be served).

Planning for Tomorrow

A fourth model which is useful in some situations and which parallels the planning-from-strength model can be described very simply as "getting from here to there." This model focuses on three questions: What, in our understanding, is God calling this congregation to be and to do five (or six or four) years from today? Where are we now in relationship to where we should be five years hence? How do we go about getting from here to there? This is a very strongly goal-oriented model and resembles the concept of management by objective. It requires the people to dream, to envision the future, and to focus on the potentialities. This helps define "where we should be five years from now." Second, it requires the people to identify contemporary reality and to recognize both the assets and the liabilities of today. Third, the process of getting from "here" to "there" requires planning, policy formulation, decision-making, decision implementation, and evaluation. In very simple terms this process can be described by this diagram:

Nonplanning

The list of planning models that might be used by a congregation is very long, and it is impossible to describe them all here. The list includes the system developed in the United Presbyterian Church as "Planning-Budgeting-Evaluation," the use of the church budget as the beginning point for analysis, reflection, and planning since it is usually the place where influential planning has been happening.[1]

There is no one "best" model. Which is the best model to use will depend very heavily on local conditions at the time that a serious planning effort is undertaken. Among the least helpful are planning from weakness, planning by cliché, planning in response to a crisis, planning for efficiency and economy (rather than for ministry and quality), scapegoating, planning for yesterday, and "studying the community." Among the generally useful planning and decision-making models are management by objective, planning from strength, planning for tomorrow, cost-benefit

---

[1] For an elaboration of this model see Lyle E. Schaller, *Parish Planning* (Nashville: Abingdon Press, 1971), pp. 36-64. For other very helpful approaches to congregational planning models see James P. Anderson, *To Come Alive!* (Philadelphia: Pilgrim Press, 1970); Marvin T. Judy, *The Parish Development Process* (Nashville: Abingdon Press, 1973), and Lyle E. Schaller, *The Decision-Makers* (Nashville: Abingdon Press, 1974).

(allocative), innovative, from-purpose-to-program-to-performance-to-evaluation, planning-budgeting-evaluation, from old role to new role to new goals,[2] policy-planning, and the "here-to-there" model described earlier.

Regardless of which model is used, however, there is one concept which should be kept in mind and which can be integrated into most other models. Identified by its critics as "nonplanning," it can be described by contrasting two approaches. While the first is a caricature, it is not as much of an exaggeration as it may first appear. Back in the late 1940s and early 1950s, if one judges by actions rather than by the rhetoric, much planning was apparently based on the assumption "Never again will we have the wisdom, the foresight, and the talents of so many gifted people assembled in one place as we have here today. Therefore it is our responsibility to make all the decisions now on all questions which may arise during the next quarter-century because those poor folks ten or twenty years from now may not have the benefit of our wisdom."

At the other extreme is a view represented by the statement "We do not know the needs of the people who will be here ten or twenty years hence, so there is no point in our trying to plan for tomorrow."

Between these two extremes is a view which is reflected in this statement: "We do not know the needs, the values, and the wishes of the people who will follow us. We do know, however, that they will probably want to do things differently than we do now. Therefore let us plan in such a way that we leave the optimum range of choices open to those leaders who will follow us here so they can make use of what we do but also have the flexibility necessary to change and to adapt to the needs of their day." The Akron plan of church construction which flourished in the 1870–1925 era is one example of the first approach. The

---

[2] For an elaboration of this concept see Lyle E. Schaller, *Hey, That's Our Church!* (Nashville: Abingdon Press, 1975), pp 160-77.

flexible and multiple-use worship facilities being built in the 1970s represent this intentional "nonplanning" model.

While the shape of the administrative structure and the intentional selection of a relevant planning model are influential in creative church administration, most leaders, sooner or later, will raise the question "But how do we motivate people?" That is a related question, and to some extent it is influenced by organizational forms and the choice of planning models. This question on motivation deserves a separate chapter, however, since it is an essential element of creative church administration.

█▌█▌ Motivation

How do you help people to become what they can become? How do you get them to do what they can do? Why do people do as they do? Why don't some people do as we feel they should do? Why does the same effort to motivate people "win" one time and "lose" another? How come? What about our efforts to get them to do the things we try to get them to do—to become, even to come (attend), to work, to serve, to grow, to give time, money, or other resources, to "cooperate"? What is a Christian view of motivation? How do you get people to do what they should for their good and for the good of the "cause"? How far should the Christian pastor, other ministers, and church leaders go in attempting to influence people?

These questions and many others like them haunt ministers and other church leaders almost daily—and sometimes nightly! One who really had sufficient answers to such questions would stand as the great leader of our age.

The predicament of many was voiced poignantly by one perceptive Baptist pastor when he declared to his congregation, with positive intent and emphasis, "You have called me to lead you to be and to do what you know in your hearts you ought to be and to do, but don't want to. You will be unhappy with me if I don't make a good try. You might be unhappy with me if I succeed with you. Try I must. Please pray for me, and for yourselves."

Perhaps the best way to begin is not with a definition of motivation, but rather with a definition of creative church administration. A useful operational definition can be stated in these words: *Enabling the children of God, who comprise the Body of Christ, the church, to become what, by God's grace, they can become, and to do what, by God's grace, they can do.* The general church leaders—pastor, minister of education, other ministers with administrative responsibilities—serve an enabling function. The enabling they do is the human part of a partnership which, coupled with the enabling of the Spirit, comprises the leadership quotient in the church context. Other church leaders relate to the enterprise, in addition to the ministers. Their work is of an enabling nature, too. Together the leaders in a church make up the ministry of administration.

Motivate or Manipulate?

Put simply, a motive is what causes a person to act or to react. Motivation is the act of unleashing that within the individual which incites him to act or to react. When the unleashing is stimulated from within a person we call it intrinsic motivation. When the stimulus is generated from without, as would be the case with the use of incentives, we call it extrinsic motivation. Intrinsic motivation, which many feel to be the purer kind, is like impulses or springs, often unrecognized or unconscious, providing impetus or driving power arising in oneself. Extrinsic motivation, considered by some to be less preferred in terms of ethics, is like an inducement, a spur, a goad, or an incentive, stimulating from outside oneself the internal impetus, causing one to act or to react.

For a minister or a church leader to attempt to touch some inner trigger in another person that would set off an impetus to act or to react can be risky. You might violate a person's sensitive psychological territorial boundary, creating resistance or resentment (or both). Or, if the motivator succeeds in getting his own desired response, the result might be manipulation.

Many, if not most, Christian leaders seem to frown upon manipulation.[1] Some see manipulation as getting a person to do something about which, if the manipulated realized what was happening, he would at the least have misgivings. There is in manipulation the attempt to use or to influence persons for the advantage of someone else or some extraneous cause. Benefits might accrue to the manipulated persons, but that would be incidental or secondary. In recent years some critics of the church have accused it of being more interested in what persons could mean to the church (survival) than in what the church might mean to persons (service). A paradox exists at this point: one could hardly kill a church bent on service; but a church given over to survival tactics seems destined to wither if not to die by its own selfish hand.

The intricate and often hazardous lines of demarcation between motivating and manipulating pose some problem situations for the minister. Is it right to do right, or to get it done, for the wrong motives? Says who? History, as well as current events in the church sector, is replete with illustrations of "good" being accomplished as a result of less than the "best" or "highest" motivation. Robert Raikes, venerable founder of the "modern Sunday school movement" in the 1780s, rewarded those Gloucester urchins who attended his Sunday school with a coin. Some churchmen today sponsor promotions with extrinsic motivators or giveaways ranging from Sunday school attendance pins to statuettes of classical composers, shetland ponies, cash, motor-

---

[1] While this chapter emphasizes the role of leaders in motivating—or manipulating—people, it should be kept in mind that the process of motivation—or manipulation—is also heavily influenced by how the congregation is organized, by the internal "reward system," by the process used to nominate individuals to positions of leadership and influence, by the choice of planning models, and by the other institutional forces discussed in the first two chapters.

cycles, and Holy Land junkets. Rumor has it that one man who had earned perfect-attendance pins each year for so many years that together they reached the floor had to miss for the first time because he broke his leg when he tripped over his string of pins!

One church in an otherwise sophisticated community has a larger item in its annual budget for attendance awards than it does for specialized leader training for the workers in its program opportunities.

Perhaps one of the truths which is apparent is that extrinsic motivators come nearer to being tools of manipulation than do intrinsic motivators. And some of the questions that remain are: What motivates the motivator, or the manipulator? Is the advantage or well-being of the motivatee or the manipulatee of utmost importance in comparison with that of the motivator or the manipulator? A fair general principle, which admittedly leaves something to be desired as an absolute guide capable of universal application, might be to determine in any given instance just who is to be the primary beneficiary of the efforts of the motivator or manipulator. Even this guideline, it would seem, should face up to the question of who is to determine what is in the best interests of a person, and on what premises. The task is certainly delicate and difficult, and should be a subject of thoughtful study for every administrator.

What Makes People Act or React?

What causes an impetus which operates on one's will and drives one to action? There are no simple answers to such a complex question. Motivation research volumes could almost fill a library. The factors seem to be too many and too varied to afford any one line of explanation.

More often than not, persons seem to act as a result of an amalgam of motives. Students of the functional chemistry of mankind at various times have analyzed persons and have discovered and revealed helpful insights into what moves

69

them to act or to react, into what makes them "tick." Like a swinging pendulum on a clock, however, there is the "tock" side. With persons, there are many, many sides. Freud spoke in terms of impulses of the aggressive, survival types, which evoke a will to live. For Adler, a contemporary and onetime colleague of Freud, the big thing was the will to mastery, the will to power. It has been suggested that some people compensate for a sense of personal inadequacy by seeking places of influence or dominance over others. Viktor Frankl articulated as the driving motive for living the will to meaning and purpose. These are among the more noted psychologically based vistas opened by leading scholars of the field.

Some students of motivation have developed very helpful schemata for explaining what makes people act or react. Among the most noted and helpful is that proposed by Abraham Maslow and commonly referred to as "Maslow's hierarchy of needs." Maslow identified man's needs in terms of physiological needs, safety needs, social needs (including love and belongingness needs), and, finally self-actualization. He affirmed that the need with the greatest strength in a given moment prompts action; and that as a need is satisfied its strength is reduced and the next need in the hierarchy becomes dominant. There is a dynamic about the schemata, and an apparent validity, which commend it to many as a constructive way of viewing what makes people do what they do. Our definition of church administration at the beginning of this chapter, emphasizing enabling persons to become what they can become by God's grace, is akin to the self-actualization level in Maslow's schemata.

Douglas McGregor's "Theory X" and "Theory Y" have shed valuable light which lets us see more clearly than before the importance of the motivator's opinion of the motivatee which prompts the motivator in his efforts to induce action. "Theory X" essentially assumes a very low view of man as regards his innate interest in and capacity for initiative in productivity (work). The motivator operating on

"Theory X" would rely very heavily upon the reward-punishment types of motivation, the carrot-and-stick image described by Harry Levinson in his provocative book *The Great Jackass Fallacy*. The assumption, consciously or unconsciously, is that one is dealing with jackasses who are to be manipulated and controlled. Of course, one inference of the "Theory X" view and the "jackass" image would have to be that motivators are people, too, and subject to the same classification. Surely no Christian administrator would be satisfied to allow himself to be so classified, either by word or by deed.

"Theory Y" assumes a view of man which is much nearer the level of acceptance for the Christian administrator. Interest in and concern for the welfare of the motivatee, such as is compatible with the historical Judeo-Christian ethic in its estimate of the worth of the individual, can be seen here. A "Theory Y" leader would assume, among other things, that a person wants to do a good job, and to complete his or her tasks. Such assumptions seem to be valid premises for the Christian administrator, and will appear in an approach offered near the end of this chapter.

The description by Gordon Allport (late of Harvard) of altruistic motives—the desire to serve others, or God, the desire to leave a noble memory of oneself—seems for Christian administrators an especially fruitful view, whether in dealing with oneself or with others. Commitment to and love for Christ, his people—the church—gratitude for his unspeakable gift which puts us so in debt that we could never fully repay him, should be motivators of administrators and of those with whom they work. A professional study of a sample of leaders in church program organizations in churches cooperating with the Southern Baptist Convention revealed that the "feeling of serving God through his church" was the leaders' greatest source of satisfaction in service.[2]

[2] The complete report of this study, "Adult Leadership in Southern Baptist Churches," is in the Data-Dex Collection, Dargan-Carver Library, 127 Ninth Avenue, North, Nashville, Tennessee 37234.

71

Such service, with its accompanying satisfactions, is inspired for many people by their love-faith commitment to Christ, which causes them to want to serve him. The definite "in-good-taste" appeal to the emotion of love seems well in place as a reservoir that should be touched upon by the Christian self-motivator and motivator of others.

A cardinal principle of motivation in and out of the religious sector is that there is a correlation between the worthiness of a cause and the willingness of persons to give themselves to it, along with their resources. With the most worthy of causes, why aren't people running over one another to give themselves and their resources to the cause of Christ and his church? One part of the answer, it seems, has to be that administrators often fail to identify and to clarify the cause or causes to themselves and to their constituency. There is a tendency to become entangled, even enarmored, with the intricacies of ministries implementation—program development, organization design, providing human, physical, and financial resources, and other important means—and to neglect to set forth a clear and attractive view of the *end* for which all these *means* exist. End-means inversion has been a hazardous trap for many church leaders. It is not "safe" to assume that all know or are agreed upon the great ends toward which the church, a church in a particular place, should be moving. Identify, clarify, and communicate worthy causes and watch the support level of participants rise significantly in your church. The last section of this chapter will include additional reference to these ideas.

Many people are motivated by the feeling that they are needed, and that they can, indeed, personally make a difference. One veteran educational minister in a large city church indicated this as his most "productive" appeal to those he called upon to invite to local church membership during many years of unusually successful outreach-enlistment ministry. As he helped people feel they were needed, they decided to unite with his congregation. An increasing number of "church-shoppers" state very categorically that their "need to be needed" is a major factor in their choice of a church. They pick the congregation which persuades them that their time, energy, prayers, talents, and presence are needed in that church. Is this manipulation? Or motivation? Or an example of a response to the call to stewardship?

It would be a mistake, if not wrong in an ethical sense, to dwell exclusively upon the idea of the church's need for people to attend, to join the membership, to give their resources, and to serve, without honest evidence of the prior concern of the church to meet the needs of those it seeks to recruit.

Many a church promotion has been geared around a competitive, status-gratifying motif. "Let's beat Calvary" is a theme which has spurred many to work toward goals which were more lofty than the motivation. Others have magnified the sense of obligation as a motivator: "You *ought* to witness." Someone has said that the word "ought" is a contraction of the words "owe it." So, "As a Christian you owe it to do certain things." Surely none would deny the validity of certain basic Christian obligations. We might hope that one who is motivated by the oughtness impetus would come to have other operative factors in his motivational makeup.

Dispensing information, giving the facts, the appeal to reason, is an approach that seems to stimulate some to action. An informed constituency has about it a stamp of democracy which goes to the deep roots of thought and feeling in our complex culture. There is a facet of the human dimension which calls for an informed rationale to convince persons to act. Some seem to think, probably erroneously, that people act largely on the basis of reason supported by facts. Some of the problems with this view are clear. In addition to the witting or unwitting distortion of facts, not to mention the selective use of facts by the motivator, there is the tendency on the part of the motivatee to respond more to his perceptions of the facts—and to

73

his feelings about those perceptions—than to the actual facts themselves. The Christian administrator must give attention to facts, with integrity, in his efforts to motivate himself and others. There will be more about this idea later in the chapter.

Although any treatment of what makes people act, or react, must inevitably be incomplete, some types of motivation seem to warrant being identified and, one hopes being put down as beneath the Christian administrator's ethic. Among these would be the administrator's manipulative use of fear, intimidation, threats, and intentionally erratic and unpredictable behavior. Unfortunately the records of many churches and church institutions and agencies are not without the blemishes related to the abuses of opportunity, even of power and authority, represented by these sub-Christian and un-Christian actions on the part of administrators. And in many instances of such abuses, there seem to be few if any good alternatives to "letting nature take its course" as a solution to the problems generated. The agonies of trying to deal in a Christian manner with the non-Christian actions of a person in a position of administrative responsibility who has violated their basic assumptions and their trust make grown men and women cry in sorrow and frustration. Even policies and procedures facilitating the removal of an administrator from office are little more than expedient solutions, and usually leave permanent scars.

Would You Believe a Demotivator?

The flip-side of what motivates people might bear playing once through. Demotivation is perhaps just a type of motivation—motivation which backfires, or that doesn't motivate in the way hoped for. Some people seem to be motivated to respond with intentional indifference. Sometimes in church administration they are apparently motivated to "stand pat" and not to move in the directions the leaders want.

Others are even motivated to resist. There are times when motivators should perhaps thank these people!

It is demotivating when those called upon to respond sense that the leader's concern is not for their own interests or well-being, but rather for his own advantage. People seem willing enough to allow the leader a legitimate advantage if there is a sharing of the benefits. But eventually, if not soon, there comes a weariness with being used in a utilitarian sense, being manipulated with little or no sharing.

The administrator's real or imagined lack of integrity is a motive-quencher in others. Someone only has to be suspected strongly of dealing lightly with truth to lower or to eliminate the motivation of those with whom he relates, especially in Christian circles. One sensitive and able Christian leader remarked of his former supervisor that he was not consistently honest. "He might not tell you an outright lie; but he will knowingly lead or allow you to assume and to act upon certain premises he knows to be inaccurate or untrue to the facts. Then, when you run into difficulty because of this, he will deny that he ever said anything to lead you to the wrong conclusion. You are left conspicuously out of position, alone." Such brinkmanship with truth seems too dear a price to pay or even to risk in a Christian enterprise. Knowingly and intentionally allowing untruth to go as truth is only a different form of lying. Any intense student of biblical truth should be impressed with the manifold condemnations of lying evidenced in the Bible, along with the promise of the direst of consequences in store for the unrepentant, unforgiven liar. Hopefully those who succumb to the many pressures to succeed, to get ahead in the various statistical and other competitions, and who as a result falsify the records or sanction such falsification, or engage in other forms of deceit and dishonesty, will seek and find forgiveness.

Playing games with followers can demotivate some of them. One such game is the "How long will it take you (clods) to guess and to 'approve' what the predetermined decision is?" game. The length of time spent in some committee or board meetings is affected by this game. One committee member, upon discovering himself to be in a situation like this, had the courage to tell the chairman never to invite him to another committee meeting to spend his time guessing at a decision that was already determined.

Another demotivating game some administrators play is "You suggest ideas, and I will tell you how stupid you are." After a while one has the inclination to say, "Okay, it's your turn: you suggest some ideas while I shoot them down." The best contributions may never be offered if a person is clobbered as fast as he produces ideas. Every administrator stands to benefit from a continuing study of creative problem-solving through brainstorming, such as is advanced at the University of Buffalo as an outgrowth of the work of the late Alex Osborne.

Some play the game of pretending to desire suggestions from participants, but then making it difficult or impossible to get a suggestion to the right person or place. A cartoonist caught this idea in a single drawing showing a person in an office trying, without a step ladder, to reach the opening of a "suggestion box" which had been placed near the ceiling of a ten-foot-high room.

Many other demotivator situations exist. Some administrators experience "hardening of the categories" in which they put people. Generally, a person finds himself in a lower category than he can accept, with little or no chance of improving his slot in the mind of the administrator. Eventually the categorized person may come to feel that he should not disappoint his leader by failing to live down to the restricted, usually low expectations.

Too many responsibilities placed on too few people was a factor identified in one research project as the greatest source of discontent among workers with church groups. Sometimes the eventual outcome of this practice is that the participation and even the membership of some of these persons are lost. Expecting too much from too few seems to underwhelm some of the participants. An administrator who is genuinely interested in trying to enable persons to become and to do what they are able, by God's grace, to become and to do, will attempt to avoid or to overcome these and other demotivators, such as the hidden agenda, embarrassment, and undeserved or insincere praise. (The demotivation process is also frequently a byproduct of several of the forms of self-defeating behavior described on pages 47-54.)

How Does an Administrator Motivate Creativity?

Churches do "pitch" toward various response "buttons" in their attempts to influence persons. We see the gamut of Maslow's hierarchy of needs in the appeals of the promotional materials and slogans churches use. And who is to say that it is bad to appeal to physiological and safety needs by letting people know that church facilities are air-conditioned and the nurseries are sanitized? Shouldn't they be? And isn't it OK for a church to be known as a friendly church—thereby assuring people that it is interested in their social needs? The slogan "The Church Where Everybody Is Somebody" might be improved by using "a" and not "the," while still assuring people of the church's interest in encouraging high esteem for persons. How would it be to advertise as "A Church Committed to Helping You Become and Do What You Can, by his Grace"? A church which could live up to this ideal would be operating on the self-actualization plane—helping persons to become what they potentially can become.

Perhaps a personal model would be fitting at this point— not a perfect model, but a model that might move us in a worthy direction and toward a worthy outcome.

A Christian administrator-motivator must begin with himself. Avoid the negatives, the hazards and traps previously described. Take a "baptized" "I'm OK" position regarding

77

yourself: "I'm not perfect; I can err, and sometimes will. But I am made in His image, and that's far from being junk; and with His help I am moving in the right direction."

Make or remake a personal policy decision: be honest, with God's help, with him, with yourself, and with others. In this honesty, do not be crude or indiscreet.

Generate and identify with worthy causes. Remember there is strong and positive correlation between the worthiness of a cause and the willingness of persons, both yourself and others, to support it. Avoid identifying with or generating unworthy causes, and the pretense that all causes are of utmost or equal worth.

Behave consistently and predictably. Avoid intentionally erratic or unpredictable behavior. Develop and maintain integrity between what you say and what you do.

Communicate to the best of your ability. Communication is any form of behavior which results in the exchange of meaning. The whole person communicates. And there is limited if any motivation without communication. Communicate the truth, the facts, with integrity.

Be an example. Try. Let your example be good, positive. The "Follow Me" on the shoulder patches of the officer-candidates at Fort Benning, Georgia, should be the figurative symbol of the Christian administrator-motivator.

Look at people positively, individually. Take a "baptized" "You're OK" position regarding all other persons. They are made in His image, too. Take the initiative appropriately to convey that you stand ready to help them do what they see as being in their best interest, insofar as is right and feasible.

Put the need of the individual on a par, at least, with the task you might be influencing him to relate to. Try to integrate the person's goals legitimately with those of the church or organization. See his advantage as a prior concern. Avoid using people for your advantage rather than seeing their advantage. Be conscious of what's in it for them.

Assume that a person wants to do a good job, to complete his tasks—Theory Y. Even when someone has difficulty doing his job well, assume that he *wants* to do it well until it is thoroughly proven otherwise. And do what you can to help him succeed in doing a good job.

Invite and accept people's genuine participation in group enterprises, even (or particularly) in the significant planning stages. Listen. Hear what they have to say. Avoid clobbering an idea just because it appears unsuitable. Call for more ideas, defer judgment, and lead the group to select the best possibilities after ideas stop coming. Someone whose early suggestions are really of poor quality might come forth with some good ones if you don't beat him down at an early stage, by premature or personal rejection of his suggestions. Other benefits accruing from such participation include the participants' increased knowledge of the task, increased personal identity with it as their own, increased value estimate, and increased communication potential, all of which result in more and better support.

Work with the opposition. Realize that a normal and natural response to many attempts to motivate is at first negative. This can be good, for many reasons. For one thing, the opposition is sometimes right! By listening to (as opposed to crushing) the opposition, you could be spared some costly mistakes. Then too, if you fail to hear the opposition through, you risk others suspecting that the opposition might have been right. Again, it is often true that the more the opposition speaks, the more clear it becomes that they are in error. Also, unless you are extremely careful, if you fail to let the opposition clarify their view, you risk losing them not only for the present, but possibly for the future too. All in all, opposition may help produce a product (program, building plan, etc.) that is better than that which would have been produced without the opposition. Opposition makes "position" sharpen its tools. Even if the opposition has to be outvoted, they may have made a contribution by stimulating those in "position" to develop a better, clearer idea.

Put it all together. Develop clear goals for yourself, and with others. Let your goals be within the range of challenge: low enough to be reasonable, with more than routine effort; high enough to require worthy but possible effort and still be reachable. Let the goals meet people's needs at the levels of their needs, and beyond, until the highest needs are met.

Clarify expectations, standards, with persons involved. Take time for understanding to develop. Worthy endeavors, particularly with others, require time.

Show interest in and awareness of progress, whether in personal growth or in a task. Approve. Give appropriate recognition, in private and/or in public. Give sincere and deserved praise. Learn to say "we" instead of "I," particularly when speaking of accomplishments shared in by others. Say "Thanks" as often as it is deserved. It doesn't cost much, but it's priceless.

Run against your own clock, and allow others to do the same. Some years ago a coach who accompanied a track team to the Olympics, where they were beaten badly, commented on the difference in mental attitude between the winners and the losers. He pointed out that the members of the winning teams, in their training for the big events, were forbidden to pay attention to where the other runners were in their progress around the track. Instead, each runner was to run against the clock, as though there were no other competitors in the race. Perhaps unconsciously, those who trained by pacing themselves against the other runners, being satisfied to come out even with or slightly ahead of them, had difficulty when called upon to run against the clock and beat records.

Isn't the Christian race a matter of each one trying, with God's help, to become and to do what he, himself, can become and do? The Christian administrator does not try simply to motivate people to do things. He tries to enable them to unleash their motivations in order to fulfill their capabilities. He who does this will be a creative motivator. And then he can say with the apostle Paul, "Therefore, having this ministry by the mercy of God, we do not lose heart. We have renounced disgraceful, underhanded ways; we refuse to practice cunning or to tamper with God's word, but by the open statement of the truth we would commend ourselves to every man's conscience in the sight of God" (II Cor. 4:1-2 RSV).

In addition to the institutional pressures on motivation described in the first two chapters, and the pastor-administrator's role as a model and his leadership style discussed here, there are two other factors which are related to the motivation question. The first is enlisting and developing volunteer lay leadership in the church. The second is providing the opportunities which will stimulate creativity, participation, and a sense of ownership of the goals. Each of these merits a separate chapter.

IV Enlisting and Developing Volunteer Leaders

"We can't seem to find the dedicated people we need to teach in our Sunday school." "It used to be that if you asked someone to accept a leadership role in the church they were flattered. Now we go out and beg and plead with people, but half of them turn us down." "We can't get people to volunteer the way they used to do years ago. I guess people aren't as committed as they used to be." "I had two workers on the line to work in my division, but when they learned of the new couples' class being formed, they backed out."

Does this sound familiar? Some of these lines are as fresh and original as the conference last evening with a group of people responsible for enlisting lay volunteers. One recruiter reported to the group on his lack of success in enlisting a prospective worker, unwittingly using a revealing malapropism: "I contacted Mrs. Jones about taking that department of third-graders, but she *reclined.*" It seems that a lot of people are "reclining" these days when called upon to work in the church ministries!

What about this thing of enlisting and developing volunteers? Why don't we scuttle the use of volunteers and *employ* people to do the jobs in the church? Wouldn't there be better teaching if we had professionals? How did we get into the volunteer business, anyway? Everybody else uses paid help, don't they?

The largest dependence upon volunteer workers is found in the area of education ministries, particularly the Sunday school. Historians generally identify the Robert Raikes Sunday schools of the 1780s in England as the origin of the "modern Sunday school movement." It is true that Raikes, a wealthy Christian philanthropist from Gloucester, paid the teachers in the earliest of his schools. He also paid the pupils. He even provided in his will for a tasty treat for the numerous children who would attend his funeral. But there are evidences that this movement might not have gotten off the ground had not another influential layman, Baptist William Fox, and the great founder of Methodism, John Wesley, championed the cause of using nonpaid workers—volunteers. (Don't you agree that people as intelligent as we are ought to be able to come up with a better designation than "volunteer"? Didn't you, Pastor, volunteer?) The early Sunday school movement began its massive growth just after they stopped paying the teachers and used their money to furnish Bibles for the pupils to use. How much money would be siphoned from the churches' ministries allocations today if we tried to pay people for the tremendous amount of work presently donated through the ministries of the churches? Incredible, isn't it, that we should give that a second thought?

There could be better teaching if we had paid teachers in church. But there is also the possibility that the teaching would not be any better. One thing is certain, however: there would be much less learning! Consider this premise, in the form of a question: Who learns more in the teaching-learning situation, the teacher or the pupil? Have you prepared to teach a group lately in Sunday school? Or try this question: What is it we need to try to teach and learn in the church education ministries? If we are only concerned about cognitive teaching and learning, why not develop our own version of "Sesame Street" and use the tube as our medium? Then a select cast of professionals could do the entire job. There are, however, many who feel that,

83

though a limited amount of professional help may be necessary, our chief hope for changing the way people feel and behave does not lie with an all-pro corps, but with many nonpaid leaders and teachers, struggling, learning, helping one another in the pilgrimage. One of the most important educational contributions of the volunteer Sunday school teacher is that he or she serves as a model to other people!

The churches aren't the only organizations dependent upon volunteers. There are hundreds of thousands of groups in this country which use the services of volunteers—and many with admirable effectiveness. This is particularly true of organizations in the fields of health and welfare, political groups, fraternal groups, civic organizations, and veterans' organizations. A notable example of the use of volunteers outside the churches is the large use of youth, even teen-agers, by many interests. Outstanding in this regard is the use of teen-age volunteers in many hospitals. A significant number of these young people later choose a related health-care vocation. Some studies on church-related services strongly indicate that the same thing happens with the church youth who are given responsible positions involving service in addition to their peer-group activities. One study of missionaries under appointment revealed that approximately half of them had experienced a convincing call to mission service during their mid-teen years—and half of that group were at that time in a position of responsibility, performing volunteer service through their church! Perhaps churches should create a larger number of meaningful volunteer service opportunities for youth, in addition to the peer-group activities in which the youth are the object of the ministry efforts.

More church members, not fewer, need to be enlisted and developed for significant assignments in church ministries. They need guidance, and other kinds of help. Professionals in the churches need desperately to find ways to get on with the job of multiplying the volunteer work force, supplemented by a proportionate growth among the ranks of the professionals who must lead in the recruitment and development of that work force.

What Is the Job to Be Done?

The overall job of enlisting and developing volunteer workers to serve in and through the church is almost overwhelming. The sheer number of those who could meaningfully serve is mind-boggling. The recommended worker–group member ratios suggested as model guidelines by churches having the most success in their ministries efforts range from one for four to one for ten. That is to say that one person of each four to ten church members is in some position of volunteer service via the church, in these most active and growing churches. In general, the larger the number of volunteer lay workers per hundred members, the stronger and more vital the congregation and the lower the percentage of members who are inactive. Such figures relate to the total church ministries needs—teachers, trainers, counselors, outreach leaders, volunteer officers of the congregation, committee members, deacons, and workers with the many interest groups, service groups, and others. From the standpoint of human resources, few, if any, churches could operate with any semblance of their present level of effectiveness without volunteer leaders.

Enlisting and developing the many volunteers who should and could be enlisted and developed calls for straining almost every creative fiber on the part of the church's leaders. In overview, the job can be organized into five components: (1) determine the present and future need for leaders/workers; (2) identify members who are potential leaders/workers; (3) enlist potential leaders/workers for preservice training, and provide this basic training; (4) enlist members for specific leader/worker positions, and train them for these positions; and (5) provide continuing in-service training and development opportunities. Let us next take a look at each of these important facets of the job to be done with volunteers.

Identifying the Need

Church administrators and ministry leaders can determine the present needs for leaders by studying the present organization design or designs that utilize volunteers in the church and comparing the present organization with known leader-member ratios. With lists or charts of the organization design in hand, make a note of those units in the organization which require workers, and observe which of these positions are not presently filled. Full employment is the hope in a church, assuming the organizational design is adequate. General church leaders can ill afford to rest in their efforts to maintain this full employment.

Some churches are able to stay remarkably close to full employment much of the time. The beginning point is to keep current regarding the present need for leaders. Encourage division and department leaders to keep up-to-date about present and anticipated vacancies in the current organizations. Inquire about their needs regularly in the operational contacts you have with these leaders. Invite them to write notes or to call you to inform you of vacancies. Write yourself notes as you discover needs for workers.

One part of keeping abreast of the need for workers is the matter of observing carefully the attendance patterns of present workers, along with their faithfulness in giving advance notice of their pending absences to their supervisors. One alert lay leader in a large Sunday school used a very simple worker attendance report system which enabled him to know of the attendance or absence of the more than four hundred church-elected leaders in that Sunday school. He had the attendance/absence information in hand before the period ended each Sunday morning, along

86

with information as to whether advance notice of each absence was given to the appropriate supervisory person, and how far in advance the notice was given! Workers whose absences recurred, particularly with little or no advance notice, received immediate and appropriately helpful supervisory attention. Sometimes the erratic or limited attendance of a leader reveals some dissatisfaction, some mismatch of interests, or other problem factors which have a bearing on the present needs for workers.

Administrators must see and find the meaning of the symptoms of needs among workers, as did this general director of a very large Sunday school. He used a simple, colored card unlike any other report or records materials, specifically designed to give only the attendance and advance notice information. Each departmental director was trained to make this brief report directly to the general director by midpoint of the Sunday school session. The full picture could be viewed by the general director almost as soon as the last card was in hand. Follow-up was constructive, concerned, consistent. Workers' problems were solved, and workers were "salvaged" for the cause by this simple device who otherwise would not have been. This is evidence of creative work.

Determining future needs for leaders involves some knowledge of organizational design skills. Such skills require use of science, art, and a bit of prophecy. Whereas present organizational designs, studied in the light of known leader-member ratios, readily reveal present needs for leaders, looking into the future is somewhat more complex. An administrator with responsibilities that include anticipating future needs for leaders should know the optimum, minimum, and maximum leader-member ratios relative to the group or groups for which he is responsible. Different age-groups require different ratios, with attention given also to the group tasks and other factors. Suggested ratios for certain Bible study groups are fairly definite within a given age group, while those for committees and other groups might not be so well established.

An administrator needs additional organizational skills. For example, when designing an organization for which growth in numbers of members is desirable (in contrast to church committees!), one must create a structure which allows for growth as one projects the membership. To be more specific, one should determine or discover the number of members a group might reach and still be satisfactorily effective, then design the organization to begin its life with a smaller number of members, leaving room for reasonable growth before the maximum number is reached. *To launch a new group with maximum membership is to organize with a predisposition against growth!* Some might need to be cautioned, however, against beginning a new group with so few members as to discourage and demotivate. At least, when beginning a new group with meager numbers, the leader and member would do well to be aware at the beginning of the challenge they face, and to accept the challenge positively as an opportunity to accomplish the difficult, if not the impossible.

Significant almost beyond the possibility of overemphasizing is the need to take time to involve present organizational leaders in designing or redesigning the organization to which they belong. As in almost all other dimensions of planning, leaders who are to effect or be affected by changes should have ample opportunity to help plan the changes. This is true of organization design. Various leaders in an organization need to get together in the early stages of planning future organizational designs, which provide information about needs for workers in the future. With these leaders, look at leader-member ratios, prospective members, present members, and their attendance and participation patterns, sprinkle in an appropriate measure of reason and faith, and come out together with a consensus commitment, believing that what you have designed is the right thing for the need as you understand it!

Turnover of workers is a factor which has a bearing on determining needs for workers. There is a formula which some find useful in computing the actual percentage of worker turnover for a given year. Knowing the average yearly turnover of recent years is useful in forecasting worker needs for the time ahead. The formula is as follows:

$$\frac{\text{Number of resignations during the year}}{\text{number of workers at the beginning of the year } \textit{plus} \text{ the number of workers at the end of the year}} \; \textit{times} \; \frac{200}{1} = \text{Percent of turnover}$$

In churches with rapidly changing membership numbers, knowing the average yearly percentage of worker turnover could be most helpful in projecting more accurately the number of workers needed in the coming year. Those churches in which the membership numbers are fairly constant would benefit less from this somewhat scientific tool for forecasting worker needs. These churches could know the actual range of numbers more easily, since they are more nearly constant.

Identifying Potential Leaders

With at least some categoric knowledge of present and future needs for leaders, the administrator/leader is ready to move into the important area of identifying potential leaders/workers.

A good way to begin is to establish some appropriate criteria by which you would recognize a potential leader if you should see one. The criteria, standards, or job qualifications may or may not need to be formalized to the extent of having congregational approval. Some find it helpful to develop biblically based qualifications, such as those given in Exodus 18, or Acts 6, or I Timothy 3. Some add to biblical concepts certain other desirable features they would look for in identifying members who are potential leaders. Others include qualifications related to measurable factors, such as regular attendance at certain church events, financial commitment, and similar items.

Beyond a basic Christian experience and current membership in the church, however, one would need to be increasingly aware that the more items there are on the criteria list, the fewer persons there will be who measure up. It is possible to develop such stringent criteria that too few could honestly qualify. A creative alternative to a super-critical list could be to use some of the more demanding criteria as goals for workers' development as they continue maturing in faithful service.

One church was guided productively by a rather simple outline of criteria, which served as both guides and goals in identifying and developing workers. They sought persons who evidenced faithfulness, willingness, and capability. Each of these criteria they developed in more detail. For instance, faithfulness related to concerns like an evident experience of faith in Christ as Lord and Savior; faithfulness in attendance at major church events such as worship services, and regular Bible study; faithfulness in terms of loyal interest in and support of church ministries, financially and otherwise. Willingness was interpreted as being willing to accept and to fulfill responsibilities; willing to work with others cooperatively; willing to work at developing one's personal proficiencies in the particular office. Capability was construed as learning to relate effectively to one's responsibilities; and a commitment of already developed competencies related to tasks. Almost perennial development of and reference to these three suggested criterion areas, resulted in

90

a quite positive and successful potential-worker identification situation, and admirable worker development.

A church must do the work of the church by beginning with the people given to it, and helping them to become what they can become, by His grace. Don't let a desire for workers who are perfect stop you from getting on with the tasks you must address with the workers you have.

There are several techniques which can help you to identify potential leaders. One long-term approach is to develop among present leaders of groups, particularly groups of adults, a positive sensitivity that one mark of a productive group, such as a Bible study group, is that it prepares members to graduate into service. It is not becoming when a group of adults in a church hover protectively and introspectively about one another, ministering only to one another, while justifiable positions of responsibility in other areas of the church's ministries go without leadership. Adults do need to minister to one another. But one essential channel of self-ministry is ministering to the needs of others. Adults must bear the load of ministering, supplemented appropriately by youth.

At regular intervals, perhaps quarterly, provide occasions and ways for present leaders of adult groups to recommend confidentially one or two of their group members who, in the leader's judgment, may have developed to a point of readiness for some preservice training of a more definite nature than the class or group to which they presently belong offers. Do not ask class leaders to enlist their members for service outside the class, but to recommend them confidentially, after which your preservice training personnel or your church nominating group can follow up with a suitable contact with those recommended. Record the worker production record of present adult groups, and give appropriate recognition to both the groups and the leaders of those groups which produce worker prospects. For several years one Sunday school department of adults in a church with more than half a dozen departments of adults produced more workers to go out and serve than all the other departments of adults combined. This happened because departmental leaders and class teachers made this a priority goal for the department. Perhaps surprisingly, the producing department was the youngest adult department, and these are generally quite difficult to turn into producers of workers.

Another technique for identifying potential leaders is to place persons thought to have leadership potential in temporary, short-term assignments and observe their performance. Ways to do this include letting them serve in vacation Bible school, or as vacation substitutes for regular workers. Again, the leaders of the adult groups can help by suggesting confidentially those of their members they feel are ready for such service opportunities.

Some churches get good results by placing potential leaders in an associate position, to have a kind of intern experience alongside a regular worker but without full responsibility. Such an associate can render useful service to a group, can assist the regular leader, and can at the same time test and develop his own interests and competence for a regular assignment.

Many churches make good use of an inventory of members' leadership interests, talents, training, and service. Suggested procedures and materials, such as cards, for gathering and keeping up with this potentially useful data are readily available through various denominational publishing and bookstore outlets. Relatively few churches have gone far enough into this area to use computer services for efficient and effective storage and retrieval of information pertinent to their members' leadership potential. Usually the input information, for both manual and computer storage and retrieval, is gathered initially via a survey of the church members. Then as new members join the congregation, data about them is secured and made a part of the information bank. Persons interested in identifying potential leaders retrieve the information from the church's inventory.

Some system such as this is almost an essential ingredient of an effective worker enlistment and development plan.

These and other ideas can help you identify potential leaders. Most churches probably need to use all the possible legitimate means to find leader prospects, including the traditional scanning of the rolls by preservice training personnel or by church nominating committee members, or others involved in the worker discovery and enlistment effort. One great church leader led a denomination of churches to significant advances in growth and development on the premise that God has in every church a sufficient supply of workers to staff all the warranted positions. Perhaps this is really true in your church, too.

Preservice and In-Service Training

When you reach the stage of enlisting potential leaders/ workers for preservice training and providing this basic training, you have already determined the present and future needs for personnel and identified those members who are potential leaders/workers. How will you enlist persons for preservice training? How will you provide the basic training they need to equip them for satisfying, optimal service potential?

For many churches the beginning point is clarifying the need for preservice training. Perhaps most churches still bypass such training and go directly to enlisting persons for specific positions with an approach such as "Here are the people for the class, here is the room which has been assigned to you, and here are the materials you will need. We need you. Will you accept?"

Consider a church's Bible teaching ministry as an illustrative model for our thinking, since this is the largest single area of worker deployment in most churches. What special knowledge and skills must people have before they can hope to be productive leaders in the Bible teaching program? Would you agree that a comprehensive view of the Bible would be foundational? Unfortunately, most regular "Sunday school scholars" do not have such a foundation, so they would need at least a survey of the Bible which would enable them to grasp the historical, sequential framework of the revelation, and on which they could meaningfully hang the segments of scripture they would be teaching. A short, fast survey of the Bible offers many people their first opportunity for a guided study of the whole idea of the Bible. Properly presented, this survey has a very desirable exhilarating and motivating effect on the learner which is good for all concerned.

What about some insights on how learning occurs? One scientist indicated that we know more about how mice learn than about how human beings learn! Wouldn't it be advantageous for a teacher to have some solid elemental concepts about how people learn, and about various kinds, rates, and levels of learning, and about the particular kinds of learning which are the concern of a church's Bible teaching ministry, before he or she is thrust upon a group?

And shouldn't a teacher know something of the general developmental characteristics and needs of the age group which he or she has been helped to choose, perhaps after visiting and observing representative workers and members in the various age groups from all the major divisions? It has long been observed that a better understanding of the age group taught makes for better teaching. Also, there are many benefits when prospective teachers are allowed to choose an age group that interests them. In addition to better teaching, the tenure of service tends to be extended, which in some circles is a very desirable value.

Are there basic general doctrines, as well as some distinctive ones, in which a prospective teacher should be grounded before being enlisted for a place of influence as a leader in learning? And what about some supervised experiences in teaching, in which there would be guidance in the stages of preparation, and opportunities for post-session evaluation and follow-through?

The Bible is generously sprinkled with military imagery in its descriptions of the Christian life. Would a nation which hoped for military success send raw recruits into battle with no basic training in the essentials of soldiering? Yet churches have done this more often than not. And some people wonder why we don't have better results, more victories! There is an almost overwhelming need for some preservice training for those to whom we would offer service opportunities in the work of the church!

A word of caution about the goals of preservice training is probably in order. No church can afford to postpone moving on with the task of teaching until all potential teachers are fully ready to do a "finished job." It seems wiser to set the goals for preservice training at the level of helping the teachers prepare to *begin* to serve effectively and successfully as teachers. Through continuing in-service training and development opportunities they can and should attempt to improve their effectiveness for as long as they are teachers. Some suggestions will be offered about this area later in this chapter.

Some churches are doing well in preservice training, with goals limited along the lines suggested above, with courses of study designed to extend over periods of four months. Others accomplish more, perhaps in courses lasting six months, or even eight. In either case, most courses call for two sessions per week as a minimum. Some use three sessions per week. The most common times for sessions are the Sunday school period on Sunday mornings, and the periods just prior to Sunday evening and Wednesday evening church services.

What will preservice trainees experience once they are enlisted? Let's review briefly: (1) a comprehensive survey of the Bible; (2) a study of teaching and learning; (3) developmental characteristics and needs of a chosen age group; (4) basic doctrines, general and distinctive; and (5) supervised experiences in teaching. Possible, you ask? Would you believe, actual? One pastor in whose church such a preservice training course had operated for more than two consecutive years, offering two four-month courses each year, cited this course as the prime factor which made it possible to staff an additional complete Sunday school organization, meeting at a different time in his church. This almost doubled the number of persons engaged in Bible study, without enlarging the building.

Now for some guidance on enlisting persons for preservice training. Review the suggestions about identifying members who are potential leaders/workers. They include, among other possibilities: (1) an inventory of members' interests, skills, and work experience; (2) an organized system by which present leaders of adult groups can confidentially suggest members who might be ready for preservice training, or for short-term service opportunities, such as acting as vacation substitutes; (3) suggestions as to potential workers by present leaders in need of more workers; (4) general scanning of the church membership to discover possible worker trainees. Also, present church staff members and leaders should remain perennially sensitive to the needs as they relate to members in the usual contacts throughout the year.

Best results in enlistment generally are not achieved through open invitations via announcements, oral or written, calling for volunteers. Selective invitations to particular individuals seem far more successful. These can be extended in a number of ways. Those doing the enlisting can call on potential trainees in their homes, by appointment. Individual potential trainees can be invited to come to the church for an enlistment interview. Some church leaders like to invite all potential trainees to a group meeting, where the concepts are presented and discussed in detail. Then the potential trainees are given the opportunity to enroll for training. Innovative leaders doing the enlisting can vary these and other possible approaches to suit the need.

Some ideas to consider in the enlistment contact, whether one-to-one or by group interview, are these: (1) indicate that the invitations have been issued selectively, after careful and prayerful consideration; (2) tell of the needs the church has for prepared workers; (3) outline the plans for the course, including content, approaches, time limit, meeting times, etc.; (4) establish with the group a suggested minimum number of times one should attend (75 to 80 percent of the sessions would usually be a minimum workable attendance requirement); (5) clarify the fact that completing the course successfully does not automatically commit one to a place of service, but that in all likelihood a position will be offered to those who do so (reserving the prerogatives of both the individual and the church); and (6) enroll those who want to be part of the course. Some may want to wait until another cycle of training is available, when they can arrange to give more nearly what is required for making the most of the opportunity. Accept these decisions gracefully. As for those who can commit themselves to enroll, place the study materials in their hands, compliments of the church, if possible. Make the assignments for the first session, using a complete course assignment sheet, indicating sessions, emphases, parallel reading and member assignments, and dates of sessions. You have just begun a course in preservice training for workers in your Sunday school!

An alternate approach which some churches could develop and implement would be based on the concept of individualized instruction, using learning resources kits, and programmed instruction materials, in which measurable competencies in each of the study areas are pretested and posttested, allowing each trainee to proceed at his or her own rate. The instructors would have conferences with individuals to guide them in their progress toward achieving the desired competencies. Such an approach requires skillful preparation of learning aids, in view of the relative dearth of good materials for such highly specialized training.

Whatever the approach to leader/worker preservice training, it is a good idea to give recognition to the trainees. Some churches schedule a commencement-type church service in which the trainees are honored, with certificates of completion and even regalia in some instances! Some who use certificates of completion simply award them to the individuals at an appropriate church service. Others have a graduation dinner, a banquet, complete with decorations, dinner, entertainment, recognitions, a brief speech of commendation and challenge, and whatever else seems suited to such an occasion. The point is to acknowledge the importance of a good-quality preservice training experience, for the trainees, for the church, and for future trainee prospects.

One of the advantages of having a fairly short-term preservice training course is that, after a class or two have been graduated, veteran leaders who feel they need such training themselves can be given leave to enroll, because there will be some replacement substitutes already trained to relieve them for the duration of the course. In inaugurating such a course, however, it is generally unwise to allow a rush of veteran workers to leave their posts and come into the training course. Appeal to them to assist in conducting the first few courses by cooperating in the visits of trainees to their classes and departments, and in the supervised teaching experiences for the trainees, with a firm promise that later they may take a leave of absence and complete the course themselves. If too many veteran leaders leave their places of service too early in the development of a preservice training course, some classes and departments stand to suffer, if not to collapse, for lack of leaders.

Placement

Now let us move on to a very critical step in this process—that of enlisting members for specific leader/ worker positions and training them for the positions accepted. It would put you well ahead if your enlistment for specific positions of service could be predicated upon preservice training on the part of those enlisted. In such instances, the trainee-graduate would already have narrowed the focus of his or her age group interest, and would have had some study and practice with the age group chosen. For these persons, the enlistment and training for the specific position would be made much simpler. In fact, the training could be reduced to something more like orientation for a new worker, with directions as to when, where, with whom, and with what materials to begin, along with any special considerations for the particular position. But, regardless of the presence or absence of preservice training, let's look at some of the essentials of enlisting and training leaders for specific positions.

One important principle, frequently lacking in the enlistment process, is to be sure that a prospective worker is asked to consider only one position at a time, and is being approached by only one enlister or team of enlisters at a time. Some authorized group, such as a church nominating committee, must serve as a coordinating group, a clearinghouse for determining what positions will be offered to whom, such determining to occur *before* any offer is extended to a person. Organization leaders who are seeking workers can still freely request clearance to enlist certain persons they may want; but withhold the enlistment interview until the coordinating group can ascertain that a certain person should be offered a certain position, in the light of the total worker needs of the church ministries organizations. Not to have this coordination is to invite several kinds of chaos, such as: (1) confusing a prospective worker, with the risk of lessening his esteem of the enterprise, as can happen when several enlistment interviews are attempted with several different interests, offering more than one position for consideration; (2) losing maximum service potential by having a person accept a place for which he or she is either underqualified or overqualified, but is nonetheless committed; (3) creating undesirable competition among enlisters, resulting in an assorted array of problems for

99

almost everyone concerned. These situations, and others like them, are unnecessary and undesirable.

Another principle that warrants use is to have the person make the enlistment contact who would supervise the worker should he or she accept. This can be done with all but the top level of leaders, who might be enlisted by a committee. There are numerous advantages to this idea. The enlister can help the prospective worker "own" the process by looking at the situation needing a worker with him, so that they confirm the need together. The enlister can identify and clarify the routine and the unique expectations which the prospective worker should consider before accepting or declining the offer. Similarly, the person being interviewed can ask about job particulars which might have a bearing on his acceptance or refusal. In this way there can begin that essential line of relationship between supervisor and supervisee which must be developed if the work is to be accomplished and the worker is to be developed. With such an interview behind them, they should have fewer surprises once the relationship is established. All parties can enter the arrangement more confidently, and with more reason to anticipate success in the cause.

Avoid asking for an immediate acceptance or refusal. Ask persons to take time to give prayerful consideration to the need, and to their possible relation to the need. Let them suggest an acceptable time by which to give you the answer to your offer. In the long run, time spent in this phase of the staffing process is time well spent, with better results for all interests.

When workers accept positions, it is advantageous to have them elected by the congregation. The election has a confirming effect for the worker. It also establishes that the church determines who serves, and in what positions. A church not only has the need to control at this point; it also has the right and the responsibility. The ministries are church ministries. They are designed under the authorization of the church. They are funded by the church, and supplied with other support by the church. They should be guided by the general control of the church. The workers should be subject to election by the church—and to recall by the church, in the last analysis, if the need to recall should have to go that far.

Opinions vary about the length of tenure for church positions. Again, citing the large model of the education ministries, the Bible teaching in particular, many churches think it best to elect for an indefinite tenure, with confirmation contacts with workers made annually by their supervisors to assure their willingness to continue. Others suggested a limited time, such as a three-year "hitch" in one place. In terms of the long-range development of worker proficiency, this view seems weak. A person might be just beginning to produce in keeping with his or her potential at the end of that time. To be automatically removed from service in a position in which one has begun to be highly productive seems a waste. Normal worker attrition in many churches gives more than enough worker turnovers. Workers who aren't performing up to standard should be helped to achieve, or relieved, before three years pass. Good supervision becomes the key to the success of the indefinite tenure. Supervision is made much more difficult by limited tenure, such as three years. In the area of administrative services, such as church committees, limited tenure can be quite useful, particularly if the committee members' tenures are phased to allow for experienced persons to serve along with the less experienced.

As regards training for the specific position accepted by a worker there are several areas on which to focus. Following the Bible teaching program model, a worker needs to be trained in each of the areas included in the suggested outline for a preservice training course. The supervised experiences in teaching will likely come on the job. In addition to the areas discussed in the section on preservice training, a worker needs to study the administrative design of the unit with which he or she is to work, including both internal

101

and external relationships. Clarity regarding the administrative design can facilitate the work along lines that are needed and acceptable to the overall ministries design.

The supervisor might guide the newly committed worker in a tailored training plan, beginning with the most obvious areas of the worker's needs. Usually the time is very brief for this kind of training. It tends to merge into the continuing in-service training and development, which we will look at later. In the light of the time available, the supervisor could place training materials in the new worker's hands, request that these can be carefully studied, and set a conference time for discussion of the ideas growing out of the study. A series of conferences would be beneficial. Another related approach would be to ask the new worker to complete in writing some assignments related to the materials studied. Still another way could be to provide a checklist of persons to meet, materials to examine, and special conferences to attend in preparation for actually beginning work. If the need called for it and the situation allowed, one could have some opportunities to sit in with a veteran worker to observe and possibly to assist, in order to get the feel of working, and to discover some areas where one needs help. These and other ideas are merely germinal regarding training for a specific position after one is enlisted to serve.

Support

Finally, let us look at the area of providing continuing in-service training and development opportunities. The worker is on the job. How can you help him to do what needs to be done, and to develop as a person and as a producer? How can you help this volunteer in what to him is a new and strange role?

Possibly the most fruitful approach is to give the worker good supervision from week to week as together you do the work given to you. Work with even the veteran workers to consider the needs of those with whom you are ministering, and the approaches and resource allocations—time, talents, money—that will be required to do the work properly. Plan with your workers. Give clear instructions as they are needed. Lead workers to set acceptable deadlines. Ask them about their progress in the work, on their assignments—but don't take their work and do it for them. Offer to help them do it. Invite them to call on you as they feel the need. Encourage each worker to suggest possible solutions to problems, along with helping to identify the problems. Attack the problems, not the workers. Instead of saying, "Joe, I notice you haven't made contact yet with that prospective member of your class about whom we learned from our newcomer service," why not say, "Joe, what can I do to help you enlist that prospective member of your class about whom we learned from our newcomer service?" Stay on the problem, and off the worker.

In addition to good supervision, develop with your workers some personalized plans for their individual development. Many denominations offer helps along the lines of suggested training standards, achievement guides, and other aids to on-the-job development of workers. Go over these guides with each worker, and plan some learning experiences each will engage in. Set some acceptable goals for the year with your workers in the area of their development.

Schedule needed study sessions for your own corps of workers. Clear these with the church calendar. Teach these yourself, if possible. Utilize workers to help you. If the size of the group allows, some of the best of these sessions can be conducted in your home, or in the homes of the workers. Larger groups could meet in the church building, perhaps in the area where they routinely do their work.

Encourage the scheduling of training opportunities in your own church. Use your own members as trainers, only supplemented by outside "experts." In fairly short order you can develop your own "experts," thereby reducing the dependency upon outside help. With less frequent need for outside "experts" you can use their services more judiciously, and possibly be in a better position to call on more highly competent ones when you do need them.

Participate with other churches in joint training opportunities. Exchange leaders with them; or pool your best with theirs and sponsor the events jointly. Go with your workers to training opportunities outside your own church. Make it convenient for them to attend if you can.

Include summer assemblies and conference center training opportunities offered by your denomination. Work to get some financial support in the church budget so that those who attend will have help with their expenses. Encourage by word and precept the idea of combining some vacation time with training opportunities.

Encourage creativity and initiative in the matter of enlisting and developing volunteers. Establish some significant guidelines which are warranted and fair. Operate on principles which are worthy. Work with people as though they deeply desire to serve, and to serve in some correlation with their potential. God has been able to work through volunteers in superlative ways throughout biblical history and the Christian era. Let ours not be the generation of leaders in the church who fail to use the gifts he has given us "for the immediate equipment of God's people for the work of service" (Eph. 4:12 Williams).

The equipping of the saints does not end with the placement and development of a support system, however! In creative church administration the process includes two additional steps: enlisting the help of all the members in contributing ideas and in providing intellectually and spiritually enriching experiences which will stimulate volunteers to develop new and more effective approaches to ministry.

V Encouraging Creative Thinking

"I wish we could have a junior choir again." "I wish we could have a ramp leading into the church so people in wheelchairs could attend." "I wish the minister would take a few minutes to introduce and explain the setting for the scripture lessons before he begins to read." "I wish we could have a Christmas Eve service every year." " I wish we could have at least one major congregational social event every month so the members could become better acquainted with each other." "I wish we could have at least three or four special offerings for missions every year so our people could respond more adequately to the needs of others." "I wish we could paint the sanctuary a lighter color." "I wish one of the ministers would visit the shut-ins at least once a month." "I wish we could have more joy and a greater sense of thanksgiving and gratitude in our worship services—they're so glum and dismal!" "I wish we could have a series of three or four sermons on the book of Revelation—I never have been able to understand that part of the Bible." "I wish someone new would speak to me—this is my fourth Sunday in a row as a visitor here, and the same two people spoke to me each of the first three Sundays." "I wish someone would ask the organist to play a little faster; the singing is so doleful." "I wish our young people were more interested in the church." "I wish we could give the first twenty-five cents out of every dollar in the offering plate to missions."

"I wish we could have a Tuesday or Wednesday Bible study group for young mothers." "I wish we could have a full-time minister of music." "I wish our church was more concerned with the lonely and the forgotten people of this community." "I wish we could find out what happens to our wishes."

These are representative of the comments received by churches which have *actively* sought to encourage the members to think creatively about the life, program, and ministry of their church.

Listening for Wishes

How can the leaders in a worshiping congregation encourage the members to think creatively about the program and outreach of their church?

The first step is to listen! The most effective listening occurs when *each* member is called on personally and the caller clearly expresses the desire to hear what that member has in his or her heart and mind about the church. This process requires an average of one to two hours per member. The length of time required per call ranges from ten minutes to seven or eight hours, but the caller will be most effective if it is assumed that each call will require *at least* one hour. This system requires a return call on each member, preferably by the same caller, a few months later, to prove that the person was heard, that his or her dreams and complaints were heard by the leadership of the congregation, and to report to the member what happened as a result of the earlier listening call.

Many congregations feel they cannot organize a calling-listening-reporting-back program on such a massive scale, and some of these have turned to another approach to discover the hopes, wishes, gripes, ideas, complaints, dreams, and latent ideas in the hearts and minds of their members.

Typically this procedure takes one of two forms. In the

more widely used method there is an "I wish" card in a pew rack. Some of these are 2½-by-4-inch or 3-by-5-inch cards, and completely blank except for the invitation to write out the wish and drop it in the offering plate. One form of this invitation is reproduced below.

Have you ever sat in church and thought to yourself—

"I Wish . . ."

We would like to make **your** wishes come true, so far as this church is concerned. There follow several wishes, including a place for you to put your personal wish if we haven't listed it. Check or write your wish, sign your name, and drop this folder in the offering plate, or hand it to one of the ministers.

In other congregations the "I wish" card is printed on a 5-by-6-inch sheet and folded once to make a 3-by-5-inch folder. The front of this folded card usually carries the invitation to make a wish and the name of the church. Inside the card there may be printed several alternative wishes with an invitation to check the ones which are appropriate. (An example of these printed wishes is shown below.)

☐ I WISH to become a member of a church school class.

☐ I WISH to enroll my child in church school.

☐ I WISH to become a member of this church.

☐ I WISH to have offering envelopes.

☐ I WISH I had some special task to do for my Lord in this church.

☐ I WISH a minister would call on _____

_____

_____

whose phone number or address is:

_____

I suggest this visit because

_____new family

_____illness   _____prospect

_____need help   _____other

On the inside and/or on the back of this folded "I wish" card may also be included such items as "I wish to hear a sermon on . . ." with space left blank for the person to complete the statement, or "I wish I could be given the opportunity to serve this church as a . . ." again with the space left blank for the person to complete the wish.

A large space is left blank for the person to complete the sentence which begins simply, "I wish."

An alternative procedure for soliciting the wishes of the people in the pew may be used during the Sunday worship service or at a congregational meeting or a planning retreat.

Regardless of the setting, this procedure calls for the leader (minister or chairman of the planning committee or guest leader or president of the congregation) to actively encourage those present to write out their wishes on a card or a piece of paper. It may be helpful if these three suggestions are added when the invitation to make a wish is extended:

1. Be as specific as possible; make it a wish that might be turned into reality, not a dream that can never be realized.

2. If possible, make your wish one that can become reality within the next twelve (twenty? thirty?) months.

3. If you would be willing to work on the committee or task force or group that will be needed to make your wish come true, please sign your name. Otherwise please do not sign your wish.

If the circumstances permit, it is often helpful to enlarge this procedure by adding two further steps to the process.

First, ask all the participants to identify someone in the room who might be sympathetic to their wish. They are to stand up, go over, and explain their wish to that individual. Ask them to take three or four or five minutes to talk over their wish and then rewrite it in a revised form as the result of this discussion. Allow ten to twenty minutes for this process to take place. (It is not uncommon for this to be done during the sermon period in the worship service if the circumstances are appropriate.)

Second, after everyone has had a chance to discuss his or her wish with another person, ask those who are signing their wish to seek other signatures too. It should be made clear that by signing another person's wish the signer is indicating a willingness to work on the task force or committee to make that wish come true.

Why?

Why is it helpful to solicit wishes from people? Those who have used this procedure reply that (1) many excellent suggestions and ideas have been submitted; (2) needs are identified which had escaped the attention of the leaders; (3) the signing-of-the-wish procedure opens the door to finding a group of people willing to turn an idea into reality; (4) it opens an additional channel of communication from all of the people to the leadership; (5) it allows some people to "ventilate" their pent-up hostilities; (6) the process encourages both a sense of and the actuality of a broader participation base; (7) the meaningfulness of the preaching is improved for some people as they have the opportunity to suggest sermon topics; and (8) the chance to submit anonymous wishes opens the door for the shy, the silent, and the bashful.

CAUTION: If you solicit wishes, report back what happened! This can be accomplished in several ways: at the annual meeting, in a mimeographed report on "What Happened to those Wishes" sent to all members, during the announcements, in the worship service, by a poster, in the bulletin, by a story in the local newspaper, by a special color-slide presentation at a fellowship dinner, by personal notes to people, at the board meeting, at the monthly meeting of the women's organization, through the Sunday school, by an 8mm color movie, by a large display of posters in a corridor, by quarterly one-page letters to the members, or by a dozen other channels of communication to the members. If you ask for wishes from members, use at least five of these report-back channels to help people know what happened to their wish!

Learning from Others

"If we were doing it over again, I would schedule a special meeting of the church council the same evening that we return," urged George Anderson, "I thought we would be bushed after the two-day trip, but I was really 'turned on' by what we saw and heard in Indiana."

"You're right," agreed Mrs. White. "I would have opposed the idea before we left, but if we could have come in and reported to the church council that same evening we returned, they would have caught more of our enthusiasm."

The speakers were part of a six-member delegation from an Iowa congregation, and they made these remarks several days after returning from a two-day visit to two churches of similar size and type in two different Indiana communities. The six had gathered at the pastor's home to review what they had seen and heard, and to organize the presentation they were to make to the church council the following Tuesday evening.

This congregation discovered that one of the best investments it could make (benefits vs. costs) was to open the door for several of its leaders to spend a day or two every year visiting similar congregations. This is another approach to stimulating creativity in program-planning which is being used by an increasing number of congregations.

The benefits include new ideas for program and mission, renewed enthusiasm, a new perspective for looking at their own situation, the chance to talk with other laymen on similar concerns, and a deeper appreciation of what their own church is doing.

Such an investment is also one of the most effective ways for a parish to fulfill its obligation to provide new opportunities for the spiritual and personal growth of the members.

What can you do to make this happen in your church?

First, expectations are very influential. If a few leaders believe it would be a good idea to study what two or three similar congregations are doing, the probability increases that it will happen. One congregation rotates members out of leadership positions after five years to a "sabbatical year." During this year out of office, each person is expected to participate in several in-service training events.

One small rural Presbyterian church expects every member of the session to visit (*a*) two churches of the same type and (*b*) one Presbyterian mission program, either at home or abroad, every two years.

Another congregation in January asks each member of the church council to choose the month in which he will report to the council what he learned from his visits to other congregations.

Second, it is important that the visits be made to congregations of a similar type and size. Similarities in type and style are more useful than the fact that the churches are of the same denomination. Members of a small rural Lutheran congregation would find that visiting a large downtown Lutheran parish is usually less productive than visiting a similar small rural Presbyterian or Methodist church.

Third, go at least two hundred miles from home. Visits to nearby congregations usually have less impact than visits to more distant parishes. Why? Perhaps we tend to discount what our neighbors are doing. Perhaps the planning and preparations necessary for a longer trip raise the expectations. Perhaps the distant church is perceived more objectively. Whatever the reasons, experience suggests that the increased benefits derived from the longer trip outweigh the added costs.

Fourth, never encourage a church member to go by himself. Four or five persons should share the same experience. The person going alone has no one to help communicate what he saw or learned. He doesn't even have anyone to second his motion when he gets home!

Fifth, the benefits can be increased if each person knows before leaving that he will be expected to report on what he experienced. He should be asked to do so in a manner that can be helpful to his own church as it carries out its ministry.

Sixth, it is tempting to dwell on *what* is being done in another congregation. It is equally important to learn *why* this is being done, and to discover how the persons in the host church weigh the *costs and the benefits*. The report back home should cover all three points.

Seventh, it is worth the investment of time, postage, telephone charges, and energy to select the churches to be visited very carefully. Each should be as nearly as possible a "mirror image" in terms of type (suburban, ex-neighborhood church in a changing residential section of a large city, county seat town, rural open country, large downtown, university-related) and size and type of building facility. The churches may, however, differ greatly in age, budget, denominational label, morale, program, or specialties.

It is essential that the members from both the visiting and the host churches take these visits seriously and prepare for the conference. The unannounced "drop-in" visit tends to be less productive than the one planned in advance.

Eighth, do not put all your eggs in one basket. Take out insurance. If at all possible, visit more than one church. Then, if one visit turns out to be less productive than anticipated, it does not mean the entire trip will be viewed as a waste of time.

Ninth, people making the visit should not be afraid of "imposing" on strangers. Most church leaders are flattered when they receive such a request. But visitors should be mindful of the rule of reciprocity. They should be prepared to share their experiences, successes, failures, and insights with their hosts.

Finally, plan to enlarge and expand the idea in succeeding years. One direction is to increase the number of members who get out to see what other churches are doing, and to increase the number of congregations visited each year.

Another rewarding means of expanding this concept is to encourage a half-dozen or more laymen to go see what the church is doing in another part of the world. Often this turns out to be easier to accomplish than anyone dreamed.

What did the members of the Iowa congregation feel they had learned from their visits? "I realize that we have not learned the value of failure," commented Mrs. White. "We have been so concerned to succeed and to measure success in numbers that we have camouflaged our failures. That church learned more from its failures than we have from all our 'successes.' "

"I've changed my outlook on church finances," added George Anderson. "Instead of having our finance committee cut the budget according to what we think the congregation is willing to do, let's explain the program more effectively and tell the members what we need to carry it out. That's what one church did, and it worked."

"I got more ideas about outreach into the community from this trip than from all the committee meetings and workshops I've attended in the last twenty years," said one woman. "What's more, I got to talk with the people who are doing it—and learned what to do and what not to do."

Another member of the group remarked, "If I were making the trip over again, I would take more material about our church to share with the people in those two churches. If we had been better prepared, we could have been more helpful to them. The conferences were really two-way streets."

Bob Rogers looked at the group with a wry smile. "I went along as the driver," he said. "That's all. But I found myself getting involved. Now I want to help new things happen around here."

Taking a trip such as the one described here can be both stimulating and enjoyable. At some point, however, some people have to sit down and tackle the more difficult and less exciting task of developing a plan for the total ministry of the church.

113

VI Developing a Church Ministries Plan

Does the idea of developing a church ministries plan bring images to your mind of a mad scramble of people with vested interests vying for choice dates on your church calendar, with you caught among them, trying vainly to keep some semblance of order? Or, does it call to mind a rather humdrum routine of doing year after year one project after another, merry-go-round fashion, for little better reason than that it's the time of year again to do certain things you did last year, and the year before that? Or, worse, does it bring some twinge of trauma because you have time on your hands, and you privately wonder what in the world might be something good to propose that would be fitting for your church to do?

Is your church's ministries plan determined helter-skelter, on the basis of which organizational leader or interest group gets to the official keeper of the church calendar first? One minister recalled this as one of his problem-causers in the earlier years of his ministry. With some evidence of pleasure in recalling a happening from which he had recovered sufficiently to enjoy remembering it, he told how year after year, the Sunday school director and the church training director would almost race to his office to reserve the choice dates they wanted, only to discover that the director of the Woman's Missionary Union had been there several days or even weeks earlier and blocked out prime weeks for her organization. Each year this "race" was repeated, beginning a little earlier every time, but always with the same outcome, until all realized how funny that "unprocedure" was. After several rounds that way, these mature people finally found ways to get together and schedule their major events as if they were on the same team, rather than in unproductive competition.

Is your church's work plan comprised of rather dull reruns of events which seem more like going around in circles than like making progress in certain directions? Is it like a merry-go-round, only with each year's promotion of the items scheduled requiring more color and louder music to get the same results, or less? Wouldn't it be fun to find the energies spent on going round and round being used to move you forward as a church, toward some worthy goals and objectives, meeting the needs of persons which it should be your church's business to meet?

Are you still laboring under the unbearable burden of feeling that you are the one who should come up with almost all the program ideas for your church, and that if you don't come forth, you will not be living up to the expectations the members have concerning you? No person should have to continue for long to feel expected or compelled to come up with most or all of the answers to the program problems in any church single-handedly. The gospel at this point is that you don't have to do it this way. Indeed, you can't. It is too much for you alone. Share this load.

A church's program plan—call it a ministries plan, work plan, or something else, if you don't like "program"—is the business, humanly speaking, of every member of a church who will participate; and should be the business of all the rest. For a church ever to become what it can become and to do what it can do, with God's help, administrators— pastors, educational ministers, and other church leaders— must find and use ways of developing the church's program plan that incorporate the best thinking and the largest possible participation of the members.

115

A *church* should have a program. And if it is truly the church's program, it will be more than it would be if it were the product of one person, or a few. It will likely be better. It will have the profile identity of more than one person. A leader can and should influence the church's program development, without unilaterally dominating it to such an extent that outsiders can tell "whose church" (the Rev. Mr. Jones' church) it is just from his obvious features superimposed on the program profile. Individual ministers and leaders come and go, naturally. But the work of a church needs to move on. To be sure, it should move along better with leaders present; but a church's ministries can ill afford to halt and wait, and completely regroup and head in altogether new directions, with every coming and going of ministers and leaders.

One of those funny images that really shouldn't be funny which comes to mind is of a new minister coming to a congregation and trying to "run" the church ministries planning single-handed. He might consult with a few key persons, and then, usually with much sound and fury (fizz), he goes into orbit. He makes announcements of what he has planned. He talks in a jargonese he may have learned in seminary, which few, if any, other than himself understand. He hands out promotion schemes, schedules, procedures, work assignments, that are quite good, because he did them himself. He could even use the latest psychology of colors for handouts, touted to call forth more response from the receiver. He might even include some innovative features in his plan which, though they are seldom if ever pretested, he feels sure the denomination will come to use on a massive scale, once it learns of his success with them. He probably tells his people this, so they can appropriately gauge the worth of his insightful leadership. At last the events begin to unfold with the passage of time. But these events are seldom what he anticipated. Response and participation range from nil to a few people who show up to watch the spectacle. And the disappointed, sometimes groggy, novice drags himself home, wondering what went wrong.

What Is a Church Ministries Plan?

A church ministries plan, to use a traveling man's parlance, is where the rubber hits the road. It is a means, not an end. It is a means whereby a church gives expression to its understanding of what kind of church God wants it to be, and how he wants it to meet the needs, both in and out of the church, which it is its mission to meet. It is what a church plans to do, and what it does, what it proclaims and what it believes, about persons with all kinds of needs which it is the church's rightful concern to meet.

Developing and implementing the ministries plan has great ministry potential, in terms both of process and of product. The product is important. The process of developing the product is vital. What is the product? It is a grand design for what the church anticipates doing. This grand design for ministries goes beyond the "what"—the mere identifying of program events—to indicate for whom, for how many, to what extent (qualitatively expressed), when, by whom, how, and at what cost of time, money, leaders, and other resources the church will perform its ministries. Such a product itself becomes part of a larger process which hopefully produces outcomes in the lives of persons in and out of the church, results which justify a church's existence, which make apparent its purposes, and help it fulfill those purposes.

Time spent on the planning process is far from wasted. Time spent with church leaders and members prayerfully and carefully considering why the church needs to do certain things to minister to people bears fruit in the lives of the planners in terms of Christian growth and development, as well as the joy and excitement of really coming to grips with what the church intends to do instead of just talking about ministering. Helping church leaders discover more about the nature and functions of a church that is trying to be and act like a church blesses the lives of all who are involved. Working with them to determine what you might do together in the name of Christ and his church to minister to others and to one another affords occasions for positive development to those who work at it. Even the conflicts between sincere persons in choosing what will constitute the ministries events and continuing efforts, and how you might allocate limited human, physical, and financial resources, provide opportunities for all to experience genuine Christian growth. It could just be that the most productive program of Christian education in a church is one which encourages significant participation of members in developing the church's ministries plan, and in helping to implement that plan.

To develop a church ministries plan which involves the significant participation of many persons in planning and carrying it out requires a lot of time. In fact, such an endeavor calls not just for annual planning during a period of concentrated effort, but for perennial planning. Planning becomes not just something you do, but a way of doing something—a way of ministering while planning and also while implementing plans. Like so many other worthwhile things, it takes time. It can be hurried only at some additional risk. It is, in part, an educational process. Education requires time, generally. One outstanding church leader illustrated the essentiality of time in the educational process with the analogy of hatching a hen egg. Said he, "You cannot shorten the time required to hatch an egg. You might put a blowtorch to the henhouse, but you'll only increase the risk of burning down the house. You won't shorten the time required to hatch the egg. It requires twenty-one days, and that's it."

There are ways to shorten the length of time required in some areas, however. In some nondeliberative production tasks you could increase the number of persons used with

118

some hope of reducing the time required. Again, in some tasks you could utilize the same basic number of persons routinely included, but have them work longer hours, thereby reducing the linear total of time required. Still another way would be to scale down the quantity or quality of the product. Could you guess which of these alternatives is most likely to happen in a typical church? If you guess the latter option, you have acknowledged some awareness of why some items in church programs turn out as poorly as they do. "Hopped-up" plans for church ministries carry a higher risk of poor performance than do those where sufficient time was spent on consideration of the many things that go into a well-made plan.

What Are the Benefits?

Some of the benefits of developing and implementing a comprehensive ministries plan for a church have been mentioned earlier. Let's summarize some benefits a church might reasonably expect to receive from participative program development.

You can build progress into your program, in contrast to the alternative, a repetitive, lackluster cycle of events. The plan focuses on meeting needs of persons. Certainly, some needs are relatively constant year after year, and some solutions to these needs should rightly be similar to what they were last year, and the year before. But there are changing needs. Even the same problems that exist year after year have peaks and valleys. A church ministries plan should have changing emphases from year to year in relation to the changing intensity of certain perennial problems. The same staid work that takes no notice of these shifts will not move the church forward to meet shifting needs.

You can develop continuity where it is valid and needed. An effective church program can rarely, if ever, consist solely of a series of terminal projects and special events as disconnected as beads on a string. One of the crying needs in many churches is for some sense of continuity in the work, even continuity of the structural vehicle (organization) for getting the work of the church done. Surely there is a place for terminal projects and special events; but these are most contributory when they are supplements to a continuing, progressive program and not an alternative to the mainstream effort. To have temporary projects and special events as the main work plan is like trying to operate an enterprise on the basis of exceptions rather than rules. The church calendar in such a situation takes on characteristics like those of the great spotted fever. Leaders become more like officials refereeing a melee than coaches and quarterbacks developing a game plan. Few if any continuing program efforts can be sustained in the face of a preponderance of projects and special events that do not expedite the continuing causes in rather apparent ways. When the glitter and the smoke are gone, there is little residue representing gain of either quality or quantity. Good planning is essential to producing continuity, and to appropriate inclusion of terminal projects and special events. It is possible to have good balance among these elements.

You can build unity into your ministries plan. There are many legitimate concerns of a continuing nature in a church, addressed by continuing structures for ministry, the leaders of which can work together to complement the total church effort. They need leadership and planning procedures and structures whereby they can correlate and coordinate in the planning stages, instead of arbitrating at the intersections where their conflicting interests collide, and where the ensuing accommodations seldom allow maximum effectiveness or satisfaction for anyone concerned. There needs to be a sense of the unity of a church's total effort, to which each segment of the work done in the name of the church contributes in ways which can be made evident as may be helpful. Real intrachurch unity is possible only if it begins significantly in the planning stage.

You can develop church leaders and members through their significant participation in preparing the church ministries plan. People become planners through planning. Planning skills are basic to good leadership and to good followership. Informed members and leaders emerge from planning, readier than they would otherwise be to implement the plans, as well as being better persons through the growth described earlier. It is sound leadership to develop persons through their involvement in comprehensive planning.

You can overcome some of the most difficult problem situations in church life and work while working out the planning for the church's program. High on the list of these problem situations is the need to determine priorities. In the words of one pastor as he attempted to help his congregation focus on matters of major importance in the work of their church, "There are many good things a church *might* do—but there are comparatively few things a church *must* do." Every church has some limitations on its available resources. The best churches have learned how to say no when demands outstrip potential resources! The most common areas where interests collide are finances, workers, and calendar time. The body count at these intersections is sometimes high. The time and place for priorities to be determined is in the planning stage. Some guidance for overcoming this critical situation will come later in this chapter.

Another difficult decision area which can be helped in the planning stage is that of establishing the feasibility of items planned. Many times in church programs items are scheduled and promoted with grossly inadequate attention being given to their feasibility. The capability and availability of human resources, physical resources, and financial resources can be anticipated in advance with reasonable accuracy. If there were as many abandoned and uncompleted buildings on our national landscape as there have been program items

121

scuttled by churches because of anticipatible lack of feasibility, there would scarcely be room to walk among the rubble. One of the recurring complaints heard about church leaders, even educated ones, is that they have a propensity to begin a lot of things they don't finish. Unfeasibility, along with personality and maturity problems, likely accounts for many an abandoned effort. Good planning can minimize this gloomy situation.

All these benefits, and others unmentioned, add up to a better job being done through the church's efforts. The focus is on meeting the needs of persons in the name of Christ and the church as the major control factor, in contrast to allowing a predetermined financial limitation to circumscribe your planning unduly. You decide what needs to be done, in order of priority, and then what resources, including money, you will need to do these things. If there are limited resources, those items which are thought to be of lower priority go out first. You will likely do more of the more important things you should do, and, because of higher motivation relative to the higher, more worthy causes, there will come more support and a better outcome. You stand to bring more people to Christ and church membership. You could increase members' sense of usefulness in the life and work of the church, for their everlasting good and that of the corporate body. You could increase your church's usefulness in the community and the world beyond.

What Are the Areas Which Call for Planning?

Administratively speaking, one way of identifying the areas of a church's total work design is to see it in two parts, one of which we could call "basic operations," and the other, "advance." Both of these segments require good planning perenially. To neglect either segment or area is to invite not only that one to suffer but also the other. A church which concentrates its efforts exclusively on planning and

122

sustaining its basic operations area to the neglect of the advance area will likely discover that not only is it not advancing, but it is also eroding its basic operations. Conversely, those who consider the advance area the only area worthy of a church can come to discover they have lost the base of their support, and advance dies of attrition.

Basic operations are that core of continuing, essential activity in ministry to which a church allocates a major share of its resources. One way of clarifying what this area includes is to identify those continuing, regular, somewhat routine activities that occur in your church week in and week out, year in and year out, and are taken to be just "part of the church package." Some of these are as significant as the regularly scheduled services of worship and the pastoral calls on persons with special needs. Others are as incidental as having a convenience meal for the purpose of expediting the getting together of a church committee, or some other basic group in the church. The operation of the Sunday school week after week, the training programs which operate regularly, the regular study and action groups which focus primarily on the services rendered to present members, are other kinds of activities which would be in the basic operations category.

Basic operations are basic to the survival of the church as we know it. They are basic to the church as an institution, as well as to the church's mission to nurture those already won to Christ and to church membership. A church could not function long without these essential program facets.

Many churches allocate almost all their resources to supporting and maintaining the basic operations. Unless such churches are working to reduce their allocation to basic operations while at the same time making them more effective, they are heading in the wrong direction. It is imperative that a church identify those basic operations which are sufficiently important to warrant continuance, and work toward making them serve more effectively and with reduced allocation of resources, to the point of diminishing returns.

It is critical that the base should not be weakened by erosion of essential services. This is important, like that idea from Isaiah which William Carey cited in his famous message to his fellow ministers and others, in which he spoke of strengthening the stake and lengthening the cord. He urged them to hold the cord while he went down to India. The stake, basic operations, must hold firmly if there is to be any fruitful and continuing lengthening of the cord, advance. One prominent and successful pastor who has served for more than twenty years as pastor of a great and growing university church has led that church to erect facilities adequate for its needs and priced in seven figures while at the same time leading them to increase the percentage and the amount of their gifts to missions in almost all of those years. That church's annual gift to missions is more than was the total church budget when he assumed the pastorate. During these years, the church's ministries have proliferated to meet many needs, and its professional staff is one of the more adequate staffs in the country. And advance in mission gifts is not the limit of the church's movement beyond its base.

Basic operations are as important for our planning efforts in a church as are the units of an army in battle which support the personnel who, sooner or later, must move across that hellish area of confiict and occupy new territory. Unless the troops advance there is not likely to be any victory. And if they move out without adequate support they face probable defeat or retreat, or both. But move out they must! And to win they must have support from a strong base.

Advance, as an area of a church's total ministries plan, is made up of those items which are planned to meet needs in ways not generally taken care of directly in the planning for basic operations. Some of the items which might be classified as advance are new ministries designed to meet needs of persons not previously ministered to by the church —establishing missions, new churches, extension ministries

124

to individuals or groups with special needs. These are numerous: people of another language or race, migrants, transients, people of non-Christian religions, economically disadvantaged persons, illiterates, delinquents, unwed parents, the sick, the aging, families with problems, internationals, immigrants, the blind, the deaf, the crippled, the retarded, alcoholics, drug addicts, prisoners, ex-prisoners, children needing tutoring, and many others. Some of those with unique needs are already easily located via installations or institutions within the community, such as military bases, universities, hospitals, sanitariums, nursing homes, children's homes, homes for unwed mothers, institutions for crippled or disabled persons, correctional centers, prisons, and special schools. Most churches would not have to search very far to find urgent needs for new ministries they should consider establishing.

Another area for advance, in addition to new ministries, is the extraordinary increase, within a relatively short time, of something the church is already doing. For example, for a church to plan to double the percentage or the amount of its gifts to missions in a year's time would be called an advance in almost anybody's mind. To increase the number of those engaged in regular Bible study by 50 percent in a year would surely be an advance of an extraordinary nature. To plan to retire capital indebtedness in half the time anticipated would be an advance welcomed by most if not all. To increase the attendance at the stated services of worship by 50 percent in a year would be a worthy advance. And to accomplish any of these extraordinary advances, or others like them, would require some purposeful and shared planning on the part of many people.

Along with new ministries and extraordinary increases of existing ministries, significant improvement of quality in ministries already established would be an advance. To qualify as such, the upgrading of quality should be such as would not occur without concentrated effort, and possibly the increase of investment of resources. For example, to plan to have all church volunteer workers attain a worthy minimal level of training for their work responsibility would be a significant improvement, and would lead the way to still other advances of a qualitative nature. Such an advance would likely call for a more than ordinary expenditure of time on the church calendar, and perhaps of money for training materials and for specialized leaders. Once accomplished, such an advance should enable a church to realize a significant improvement in the quality of its teaching and learning among its members and others. Illustrative also would be special plans, requiring unique effort, to improve the quality of a church's community relations by the expanding and improvement of justifiable services to the community.

Advance is whatever a church does that is right for it to do and that moves it outside the basic operations, or that significantly extends or improves the basic operations in justified ways and directions. A church needs to advance perhaps as much as those touched by the advance need the help it brings them. Surely the higher motivation is that which focuses on the needs to be met by a church which plans for advance. But the truth remains that a church is usually strengthened internally by advancing in ways feasible for it to support and to sustain for as long as the need exists. A church which has the heart to give itself away via well-planned advance could hardly give itself away to the extent that the base would be weakened. The strength gained by the missionary acts of advance will generally exceed that which is given away. This is one of the paradoxes of the faith.

With rare exceptions, advance is not the kind of church action in ministry that just happens by accident. A church must plan for advance, or it usually does not take place. Sometimes a church may seem to fall forward, advancing with little apparent effort. But then a pertinent question remains as to what sort of advance such a church might achieve if it really set out to advance. Some churches advance with apparent ease and make great progress in comparison with other churches. But when examined in the light of its own potential for advance, whose church is not falling behind the pace? A church can ill afford to settle for accidental progress. We must plan for significant, needed advance.

Who's in on Developing a Church Ministries Plan?

There is a short answer to the question of who should be in on developing a church ministries plan: every member of your congregation you can get to take a meaningful part. The "I wish" card described in the previous chapter is one way to broaden participation. Obviously, there will be varying forms of participation, and with them varying amounts of time and involvement. Avoid giving the impression that people are taking part in significant and meaningful ways, when actually they are not—like calling for members of the congregation to suggest ideas which are not going to be considered, or having the congregation or even a smaller planning group vote approval when you intend to proceed as planned regardless of the voting outcome.

There are some more specific guidelines which indicate who should be in on the intensive work of church planning. Persons who have responsibility for leading continuing church ministries which are of primary significance in the life of the church should make up the core group of planners. Heading a list based on this principle would be the pastor and other general ministers and staff members with responsibilities for leading in ministries. The general leader of each of the major, continuing "program organizations" in a church should be key leaders in developing a church ministries plan—the leaders of your Sunday school, (church school), mission organizations, music ministry, continuing training programs, and perhaps others.

The general leaders of major church ministries organizations play a role in developing a church ministries plan somewhat like that of the joint chiefs of the branches of our nation's armed services. Each heads a significant but not entirely self-sufficient force. The military branches need one another; the church organizations do, too. The hopes for developing a comprehensive, total church plan for ministries rest upon the cooperative work of the leaders of the major organizations.

The wise leader of each of the church's major organizations works not only with the other leaders of comparable responsibility, but also with the top leaders in the organization he heads. Each major church organization needs and likely has at least one level of leaders other than the general leader. Persons at this level need to be integrally connected with the work of developing the overall church ministries plan. Their primary work area is, of course, the organization in which they are leaders. But it is also the job of these leaders to help relate the work of their organization to that of the total enterprise. No church can reach its full ministry potential with its major organizations charting their own courses unilaterally, not making their complementary contribution to the total church ministries plan. The general leader of a given organization serves best who relates the work of his organization to the total effort of the church in supportive ways. To make this possible, he must lead his organization's leaders with this end in mind.

Members of a church's organizations also need to be in on developing the ministries plan. Someone who thinks the members don't have ideas and feelings about what their church does and how it does it has perhaps been unaware of the little signs here and there which might have alerted him to this truth. There are many evidences, ranging from the slight shrugs or subtle facial expressions indicating something less than supportive response when action plans are announced and members are invited (at what is possibly the first time they have heard of the idea) to join in the activities, to the little verbal asides overheard between the group gatherings, suggesting some interest they might have had if they had known earlier or advancing ever-so-gently an idea they would like to have seen incorporated in the plans. But, not having been in on the planning, they now respond with less enthusiasm, with nonsupport or something similar. Such insensitivity to the needs of members to be included in the planning stages is one surefire way to have more spectators and fewer active participants among those who do remain in the organization.

Use some imagination to think of ways to get members in on developing the church ministries plans. They can be particularly helpful in identifying and describing the needs for which a ministries plan should be developed. A growing number of churches are beginning their annual planning much earlier than formerly, and using a variety of ways of getting members to express their awareness of needs. "Town Hall" types of hearings are conducted. Group discussions at regular and extra meetings of members prove productive for many churches. Developing and maintaining a simple suggestion procedure for members to use seems basic, as does the fact that appreciative acknowledgement of suggestions offered is vital. Also, members can help in special studies, research, surveys, and other means of identifying needs and more precisely describing and validating them as needs. Information about critical needs for church ministries is more readily and more plentifully available than the uncommitted member or leader might want to know and be bothered about in his conscience! Members can help get that information. Commitment can be stimulated by means of the experiences a member might have while gathering data. Members could even become a stimulating force to encourage some leaders who might need nudging in order to get moving!

Members can help beyond the stage of identifying and describing needs. They can help with suggestions regarding approaches to meeting the needs. With their help, plus the leaders' ideas, almost any church could learn to develop a relevant ministries plan. And what a boon that would be to the churches and to the populace. People could then spend more time advancing the church's relevant ministries, and less reading books and hearing speeches and feeling either guilty or jaded about the irrelevant church! Provide sincere and workable ways for your members to suggest solutions to the concerns they help to identify and to describe and to validate.

There's more that members can do to help develop a church's ministries plan. They can help test "trial balloons." In developing plans for erecting a building, we bring before the people an artist-architect's drawing of the proposed building. They are invited to look it over, and to authorize proceeding with the plans, following agreed-upon changes where desired. Why not use this "trial balloon" idea in developing something as important as church ministries? Aren't people and their needs more important to us than buildings, if there must be a choice at that point? Give members a chance to glimpse the plans for the church ministries while they are still modifiable. Observe the correlation between their participation in the planning and their later participation in the implementation of plans.

Again, members can help by acting to approve or endorse final plans. All these kinds of participation come before the implementation stage of the ministries plan is actually launched. To avoid or evade having members participate significantly in developing the church ministries plan is not only to fail to get their suggestions incorporated into the plan, but also to deny them the great pleasure of knowledgeable anticipation of what is to come. Even grown-ups enjoy most those constructive activities and events which they can look forward to in anticipation.

Considering how rarely members are included in the ministries development process in many churches, it is a wonder that members get interested at all in the implementation stage. Someone has said that people are seldom less interested than when called upon to pursue someone else's goals. The way to make the church ministries plan their own is to allow members to play a significant part in developing the plan. And in order for this to happen church administrators—leaders in the ministries of the church—must put the inclusion of members high on their list of priorities in developing the church ministries plan.

How Do You Develop the Plan?

For many churches there are still some preplanning needs that require attention before they can reasonably hope to develop their most effective and comprehensive church ministries plan. Let's look at some of these which are common to many churches.

To have reasonable hopes of developing a highly effective church ministries plan, some churches need to undertake a thorough consideration of what it means to be a church. They need to find answers to questions like "What is a church?" "What is a church for?" "What is a church not for?" "Why not abandon church?" "What is there that makes church distinctive from other organized groups?" Such questions need to be asked and answered seriously in relation to the particular church, like my church and your church, our church. The answers should help to identify and to clarify the church's reason for existence, its purpose in the most comprehensive sense. Without the insights that can come from asking and answering—on a continuing basis—these kinds of questions, whatever plans for ministries a church might develop will fall short of the potential they could have with such insights. Veteran members need reminding, new members need teaching, and leaders need the discipline and growth that can come from keeping these questions and answers before the church perennially, and in varieties of ways, the limits of which largely depend on the leaders' imagination and awareness of the values to be derived.

131

Once the purpose of a church is more clearly understood by more leaders and members, a church is readier to develop the kind of ministries plan advanced in this chapter. In the light of the purpose, some long-term, even ultimate, objectives should be developed. The pastor together with the key leaders of the church's major continuing ministry organizations would be one good combination of people to lead in the development of these objectives, utilizing other leaders and members in ways suggested in the previous section. These objectives should benefit from biblical insights, such as the "Great Commission" (Mt. 28.19-20), and the pre-Ascension directive to "be my witnesses" (Acts 1:8 RSV). Some churches are formalizing their objectives, with the congregations' full approval. Typical of the objectives some churches find meaningful are: "Our objective is to be a covenant fellowship of Christians filled with the Holy Spirit"; "Our objective is to be witnesses for Christ both in this community and throughout the world"; "Our objective is to be a fellowship of maturing Christians whose learning results in responsible living"; and "Our objective is to be a church that unselfishly ministers to persons in the community in Jesus' name." As with the purpose of the church, the development of an understanding of such long-term objectives needs to be a continuing experience in a church, and one which is reviewed often as the church develops and implements its plans for ministries. Surely it would not be wise to wait until every detail is identified, clarified, and understood by all leaders and members before proceeding to develop the church ministries plan. The plan must be developed in the light of the insight we have when the time comes to plan. Then, as the insights come to be more clear, we need to relate them to the continuously developing plan.

The actual planning begins with discovering the needs within your church and the community you serve. The general leader group, such as your church council or ministries council, could lead in this discovery, using the help of other leaders and members appropriately. You need to get specific information of the relevant past and of the present in such areas as your church's history, its ministries, human resources, physical resources, and financial resources. About your community you need specific information about such things as who, how many, and where the people are (using meaningful ways of noticing the many clusters which make up your population), the kinds and extent of their needs, who else (if anyone) is concerned for them; and any other information which would relate to your church's responsibility for persons.

Following the gathering and analyzing of data, you will need to isolate the concerns for your church which grow out of each area of information. Write down the concerns which are isolated by the planning group. State that a certain situation or condition is a concern which your church should plan to meet, and for what reason or reasons this is so.

Concerns might relate either to the area of basic operations of your church, or to the area of advance, or to both. It will help if you identify the primary relationship. Later, when you come to consider the allocation of resources, you can get a clear picture of the balance between basic operations and advance. Have discussion and other activities that will help determine the priorities. You might rank the total list of concerns as to their priority, and also rank those in each data area. Such sifting and comparison will help the most significant concerns precipitate. It will also help assure that the scope of your concerns does not become too limited, thereby causing some imbalance in your ministry plan. Don't be afraid if leaders and members in these sessions differ in their opinions about priorities. You should be more afraid if they don't. It is from just such conflict and struggle that growth, support, unity, and many other important outcomes can be realized from the process. These sessions offer opportunities for tremendous ministry to be accomplished in the lives of the planners.

Next, set goals in each of the priority areas. These are

planning goals which should help call to mind essential strategies, action plans, and other details of a full ministries plan. Write these goals down. Make them worthy, but reachable. Let them tell for whom, for how many, to what extent, and by when a certain result is to be realized. Some planners take these goals to the congregation for interpretation and approval. This can be a useful "trial balloon" experience of the kind mentioned earlier.

Now you are ready to open the process to all levels of participation for suggestions as to what might be done to reach the goals. Don't be surprised if you get some very creative and useful suggestions, along with some very wild and impractical ones, regarding projects, events, and other activity items for the goal-oriented ministry plan. Accept all suggestions, and lead the group to judge those which should remain under consideration.

The planning leaders should pull together the church goals, with the suggested continuing and terminal activities, the projects, the special events which are most likely to lead to the accomplishing of the goals. Matters such as the calendar scheduling, feasibility considerations, sequence of emphases, major organizational changes, worker needs, and other important facets of church ministries planning call for the planners' attention. The finished ministries plan should be presented to the congregation.

The presentation of the church ministries plan to the people for their acceptance can benefit from the most creative efforts you can put forth. Let leaders and members of ministries show what the plan consists of, all the way from very vivid presentation of the evidences of needs which the planned ministries are to fill, to what approaches the activities will take, and what this means in terms of calendar time and other resources needed for implementation. It is particularly helpful to relate the appeal for financial support to the ministries which the finances will support. Later, when making periodic reports of ministries' progress, it is also valid and good to show the parallel investment of resources, particularly money, to date. Thus an otherwise routine church business conference can become a time for worshipful reviewing of what God is accomplishing in various areas of relevant church ministries, and how our continued faithful stewardship of opportunities and resources of all categories relates to these accomplishments.

Creative leadership in the development of a comprehensive and relevant church ministries plan for doing what you and yours feel God would have you do, both in and out of your church, can become one of your most thrilling and productive channels of personal ministry—enabling persons to fulfill themselves, with his help.

VII Intentionality in Membership Recruitment

Today the overwhelming majority of the adults in the United States and Canada who are not members of a non-Christian religious body have made a commitment to accept Jesus Christ as Lord and Savior. It is also true that many of those who have made this commitment have "dropped out" of the church. Whether this reflects a failure on their part or a failure of the congregations in which they were baptized or confirmed or first made this commitment is not the point of this chapter. The point here is to distinguish between evangelism—confronting the non-Christian with the fact that Jesus Christ is Lord and Savior—and membership recruitment, which means inviting people who may or may not have made an earlier Christian commitment, but who now are not actively involved in the life of any worshiping congregation, to renew that commitment and to unite with your church.

Some church members recoil at the mention of the term "membership recruitment." They translate this into "collecting scalps" or "playing the numbers game" or "head-hunting." A more creative approach is to recognize that the individual who belongs to an organization which gives meaning to his life, in which he finds the opportunity for personal and spiritual growth, and through which he is able to express his commitments, is normally eager to share the joy, satisfaction, meaning, and purpose of that organization with others and to encourage them to share in that which has meant so much to him. This may be called evangelism by some, or it may be described simply as membership recruitment. By definition the Christian is concerned about the salvation of others. The Christian who finds meaning in church membership will normally want others to share that experience.

In reviewing the alternatives before your congregation as it seeks to win others to Christ and to invite others to share in membership in *this* congregation, it may be helpful to begin by asking a few questions before moving on to examine how your church might develop a ministry directed at any one of several specific segments of the population.

The Next One Hundred?

Who will be the next one hundred people to join your congregation? Why will they join your church rather than some other congregation? After they join how active will these new members be in the life, program, fellowship, ministry, and witness of the congregation? How long will it take your congregation to receive one hundred new members? A year? A month? A decade?

One approach to answering these questions is to go back over the historical record for the past five years. Identify the new members who joined your congregation by transfers, baptism, profession of faith, or confirmation. Try to identify the reasons why these people joined *this* congregation. How many were born into this congregation or came in via parents? How many came in via marriage? How many were invited in by a person who was a member? How many sought out *this* congregation because of the program or some special appeal? How many came because this was the closest church to where they live?

Look over this record for the past five years. This will give you some idea of contemporary reality, of why people have been joining your congregation in recent years. Now ask yourself, "Will these same factors be influential during the rest of this decade in attracting new members?" If more than 60 percent of your new members during the past five years *(a)* were children of members of your congregation or *(b)* married a member and thus came in via the marriage route, your congregation will probably *(a)* decline in numbers during the next few years or *(b)* be developing new approaches to reaching potential new members.

Next ask yourself who has not joined this congregation during the past several years. How many new members have you received in any of these categories? Single men in the twenty to thirty-five age bracket? Divorced persons? Widowed men who moved to your community after becoming widowed? Widowed women? Members of minority racial, ethnic, and nationality groups? Newcomers to the United States? Older single men? Apartment dwellers? Persons living in mobile homes? How do these numbers compare with the number of persons in each of these categories in your community? If 30 percent of the people in your community are apartment dwellers, are 30 percent of your new members residents of apartments? If the eighteen to thirty age group constitutes 20 percent of the total population of your community, are 20 percent of your members in that age group? Since in most urban communities the eighteen to thirty age group represents nearly half of the newcomers, are half of your new members in that age bracket?

The next question it may be helpful to raise concerns assimilation. Who are the "dropouts" among your new members over the past decades? First, see if there is any difference between those who unite with your congregation by way of baptism, confirmation, or profession of faith and those who unite by transfer from another congregation. Which of these two groups has the higher dropout rate?

Make a similar comparison between men and women. Which group has the higher dropout rate? If a larger proportion of men drop out after uniting with your congregation, does this suggest that you have a better system for assimilating women into the life and fellowship of the congregation than you have for men? Are there more groups, specific roles, and tasks for women than for men? Is this a clue to the differences in assimilation?

After looking at the recent past record of your congregation in receiving and assimilating new members, it may be helpful to move on to look at what is emerging as the fastest-growing segment of the population. In simple terms what this means is that the babies born in that widely publicized post–World War II baby boom are now coming of age. In 1960 there were 22 million people in the twenty to twenty-nine age bracket. This represented a drop from the 24 million figure of 1950. In 1980, however, there will be 40.4 million persons aged twenty to twenty-nine in the population of the United States, compared to 22.2 million in the forty to forty-nine age bracket.

Where Are the Young Marrieds?

"I simply cannot understand why we do not attract more young married couples here," exclaimed Mrs. Roberts to some other members of Magnolia Street Presbyterian Church. "Over at Westminster there are dozens of young married couples, even though we have a better location and a more attractive building. I can't understand what we're doing wrong!"

"Relax, my dear," responded John Burt, in a soothing tone of voice. "In a few more years they'll be flocking in here, too. You know how young people are: they drop out of church when they graduate from high school, and they come back after they're married and the kids are ready for Sunday school."

"You also have to realize that most churches are in the same boat as we are," added Bob Thorp. "Very few churches have many members in the under-thirty age bracket. Westminster is an exception, but our situation is the norm today."

This brief conversation represents one response to the question "Where are the young married couples? There are five marriages being entered into in 1975 for every three back in 1960, but we have fewer young married couples in our congregation today than we had back in 1960. How come?"

A more creative approach might be to ask, "What is Westminster Church doing, and what is it we are not doing?"

An answer to the first half of this question can be found by looking at those congregations in which 50 to 80 percent of the new adult members are married persons in the twenty to thirty age bracket. There are a substantial number of these congregations, and by studying them it is possible to identify several characteristics which they share and also to build a checklist which may be used by the leaders in other congregations to review their own efforts to reach what is becoming the largest age group in the population.

Most of the congregations which have a large number of under-thirty married couples with small children offer a "package" designed to respond to the needs of this group. The congregations which have the most effective outreach to young married couples today score an "A" on at least a dozen of the components of this package, and at least a "B" on another half-dozen.

1. A weekday nursery school with a reputation for excellence, which is seen as a ministry, not as a service project, and is an extension of the Sunday church school.[1]

2. A Sunday school class for young married couples which is a meaningful group in which the members treasure their ties to the other members of the class. For many young couples who are newcomers to the community this class is the source of many of their closest friendships. The best of these groups are redemptive fellowships, educational ven-

[1] For an introduction to this program, see *Weekday Ministry With Young Children* by Martha Locke Hemphill (Valley Forge, Pa.: Judson Press, 1973).

tures, social gatherings, task forces with a unifying "project" or goal, and friendship clubs rolled into one.

3. A strong emphasis on biblical preaching. Frequently persons in this age group leave the worship service thinking, "Today that minister really spoke to my needs."

4. A program-planning process which recognizes that for some occasions there are significant differences among the members of this group which the older members refer to simply as "the young married couples." The differences include (a) the recognition that many twenty-two-year-old couples with no children feel nearly a generation younger than the twenty-eight-year-old husband with the twenty-six-year-old wife and two children; (b) the differences in schedules between the couple where both husband and wife are employed outside the home and the couple with only the husband employed; (c) the differences in needs and "freedom" between the couple with no children and the couple with one or two or three children; (d) the difference in perspective between the couple with one child and the couple with two or three children; (e) the vast difference in needs between the young two-parent family and the young one-parent household; and (g) the differences in needs and schedules between the couple who were born and reared in the community and the couple who find themselves a hundred or a thousand miles from "back home."

5. A circle or special group within the women's organization for young wives with small children—they "graduate" when the youngest child enters elementary school.

6. A staffed nursery available whenever there is *any* meeting at the church which might include young married couples. This usually means that frequently for the first year it is available but not used. It also means that both the husband and the wife can be involved in church affairs and other community and vocational events. Neither one is forced to miss a church meeting because of a conflict with the spouse's schedule. The one going to the church takes the child or children along and leaves them in the nursery.

7. An openness to innovation and creativity and few restrictions of a "but that's how we've always done it here" kind.

8. A bowling, softball, and/or basketball team for men and/or couples. Many churches have a weekly bowling league which is a means of assimilating newcomers and also for strengthening the group life of the congregation.

9. Marriage-enrichment retreats for young married couples.

10. A Bible study group for young couples, which meets one evening a week for a predetermined number of weeks, not "forever."

11. A process for selecting members of the nominating committee which *guarantees that at least two members of the nominating committee,* not including paid staff who may serve on that committee, *will be personally acquainted with each* member in the eighteen to thirty age bracket.

12. A mother's-day-out nursery one day a week.

13. Meaningful tasks and roles for husbands.

14. A drama or music group for adults under age thirty-five.

15. Periodic classes, workshops, retreats, and other events for couples with small children.

16. At least two staff members—perhaps part-time or volunteer—under thirty-five years of age.

17. Excellent quality physical facilities for babies, one-year-olds, two-year-olds, and three-year-olds.

18. One staff member—again this may be a volunteer—with specialized training in caring for the young child.

19. A children's sermon during the Sunday morning corporate worship service.

20. Two or more children's choirs (for age twelve and under).

21. A worship service held at the same hour as the Sunday school program for young children.

22. A system which helps every visitor to be greeted and identified by name, *and to be able to identify members by*

name. This is especially critical in helping potential new members become acquainted by name with the members they meet.

23. There are several different "entry points" through which new members can become assimilated into the life of the congregation and can feel a sense of ownership of the congregation's ministry, goals, and programs.

24. The operating assumption that most of the young parents who appear to be "visitors" are really shoppers. They visited a different church last Sunday, and unless there is some reason for them to return, they will be visiting another congregation next Sunday.

25. An annual all-church picnic and eight to twelve other "social" events a year which help people get acquainted with one another across age, social class, nationality, racial, vocational, and tenure-in-this-congregation lines.

26. A highly visible and easily accessible location with adequate offstreet parking for weekday and evening events and programs.

27. Perhaps the most difficult of all, there is not only a recognition but an acceptance of the fact by most of the older leaders that at least half of these younger adults will see the world from a different perspective, carry a different value system, and arrive at a different set of conclusions on most questions, than the established leadership core.

28. Opportunities for involvement and leadership by younger adults in outreach ministries to other people which cause prospective new members to think, "We are needed here. Our presence and participation could make a difference here. We want to help others, and this congregation offers us that opportunity."

As you use this checklist to evaluate what is happening in your congregation, please remember three important considerations.

First, these are among the most common characteristics of the churches with a disproportionately large number of young married adults. It is very, very difficult to find one in which all twenty-eight characteristics are present, but it is easy to find congregations which display twelve to fifteen of these characteristics and also attract large numbers of people from this age group. Is that a coincidence?

Second, a consistent theme running through more than two-thirds of these characteristics is the focus on the perspective and the needs of young married couples. This is the opposite of the frequently heard lament "The future of this church depends on our ability to attract more young couples!" The churches which are most effective in reaching *any* group of people are those congregations which focus on the needs of people rather than on the survival of the institution!

Third, in many congregations it is far easier to gain entrance into the "membership circle" than it is to gain entrance into the smaller and more exclusive "fellowship circle."

This point can be illustrated more specifically by looking back at items 2, 5, 7, 8, 10, 11, 13, 14, 15, 16, 19, 22, 23, 25, and 26 in general, and at items 8 and 13 in particular. Some readers may wonder why a church should sponsor an athletic team as part of its evangelistic outreach. The answer is simple. This is one method of (1) building friendship ties with people outside the membership of any congregation, (2) building relationships between longtime members, recent new members, and prospective members, and (3) opening one more door into the fellowship circle. The basic reason for emphasizing items 8 and 13 is that most congregations have many more doors into the fellowship circle for women than for men.

The Mature Adults

Another rapidly growing segment of the American population is the over-fifty-five age group. In 1950 there were 26 million people in this age bracket. By 1960 the number had climbed to 32.2 million, and by 1970 the total had reached

38.7 million. By 1980 that figure will be in excess of 53 million, with 30 million in the over-sixty-five age bracket.

These are impressive numbers, but they are of little value unless this large group is divided into smaller categories.

For example it is of limited value to think of developing a ministry to retired persons. It is far more productive to think in terms of these categories and subcategories:

1. Those in the preretirement period of life.
2. Those in the transition-to-retirement period of life.
3. Those in the early retirement period of life—
   (a) able and eager to travel
   (b) physically able but not interested in traveling
   (c) physically limited in what they can do.
4. Those in the middle-retirement period of life.
5. Those in the late-retirement period of life—
   (a) physically able to take care of themselves
   (b) confined to their own homes
   (c) in nursing homes and hospitals.

In looking at this "retirement group" it is critical that any effective program-planning should not place too much emphasis on chronological age. There are several reasons for this. One is that the age of retirement is gradually being spread over a longer span of years. A growing number of people are retiring, at least for the first time, at age fifty-five, while others are not retiring until they are in their late sixties or early seventies. In 1978, for example, most of the people retiring will be persons born between 1906 and 1923. That is a wide span of years!

A second reason for not placing too much emphasis on chronological age is that many people retire at least twice, and some retire three or four times. This pattern will become more common as a result of the pension reform legislation of 1974 plus the rapidly growing number of people retiring at a comparatively early age from government employment and from the military service. The number of individuals actively seeking a second career following their first retirement will continue to increase. Many of these early retirees move to a new job in another state as they pursue their second (or third) career. Thus a church might deliberately develop a ministry directed specifically at the needs of these second-career "retired" persons.

A third reason for not overemphasizing chronological age is the obvious one. At age sixty some people enjoy far better health than do other sixty-year-olds. Thus in planning a ministry to mature adults it is important to recognize the differences in physical and mental health and in outlook on life. Some seventy-year-old persons are looking to the church for a ministry of love, care, and concern, while other seventy-year-olds are looking to the church for opportunities to express their commitment to Jesus Christ through ministry and service to others.

For the church seeking to reach the rapidly growing number of young adults in the twenty to twenty-nine age bracket it is very important to recognize the many differences among the people in that age group which older people refer to simply as "young people." It is equally important that a rifle approach, rather than a shotgun one, be used in attempting to reach and minister to mature adults.

The Neglected People

Most Protestant congregations today fall into one of two categories. One category is composed of those congregations which place the major emphasis in program development and membership recruitment on serving the two-generation household. These are the "family churches" where the program is built on the assumption that nearly everyone lives in a household consisting of a husband, a wife, and two or three children.

The second category consists of the "ex-family churches." These are the congregations that reached their maximum size and strength when most of the members came from two-generation households. That day has passed, and now 50 to 80 percent of the active adult members live in one-generation households. A large percentage of these live in one-person households. In many of these "ex-family churches" a third of the addresses on the mailing list are one-person households. By contrast, in the actual "family church" only rarely are more than 4 or 5 percent of the addresses on the mailing list those of one-person households. (In 1950 there were 4.7 million one-person households in the United States. The figure climbed to 6.9 million in 1960, 10.7 million in 1970, and is estimated at 14.2 million for 1975. It is expected to approach 16 million by 1980 if the housing is available. In percentage terms the proportion of one-person households in the total housing inventory doubled in the quarter-century from 1950 to 1975.)

Many of these ex-family churches, instead of enhancing their skills in a ministry to single, divorced, and widowed adults, tend to emphasize efforts to re-create yesterday and once again become a family church serving two-generation households.

The most highly visible group of adults living alone are widowed women. The number of widowed women in the population of the United States has climbed continuously from 3.92 million in 1920 to 5.70 million in 1940, 8.30 million in 1960 and 9.90 million in 1974. One woman out of seven, age fourteen and over, is widowed. Eight out of ten widowed women live alone, while one widow in five is the head of a household with children at home.

By contrast the number of widowed men in the population has hovered around the 2 million mark for over half a century—ranging from 1.76 million in 1920 to a peak of 2.30 million in 1950 and down to 1.9 million in 1974. One out of four widowed men is the head of a household with children at home, and seven out of ten live alone.

There are slightly over 100 million adults in the United States who have passed their thirtieth birthday. Nearly one

147

out of ten is widowed *and living alone.* Eighty-five percent of them are widowed women living alone. In most communities that is a large group of people—and many of them are very lonely people, but too shy to take the initiative in finding a church.

Two other large groups who tend to be neglected by the family church and the ex-family church deserve mention.

One is the 22.9 million adults who have never married—and 6 million of them are living alone. Many of them will never marry. There are, for example, nearly 300,000 single women in the forty to sixty age bracket today whose potential husbands (in many cases, of course, the two had never met) were killed in World War II. One of the legacies of the Vietnam conflict was the death of the husbands and potential husbands of nearly 50,000 women.

In 1975 the nation's population includes 22.9 million adults who have never married, 11.8 million widowed persons, and 5.2 million divorced persons. Thus the number of single adults (age eighteen and over) totals nearly 40 million compared to 97 million married adults. Three adults out of ten are single, widowed, or divorced. What is the proportion among the adult members of your congregation?

Another method of looking at this single-adult population of nearly forty million is to divide it into three categories by age. Nearly half (46 percent) are in the eighteen to twenty-nine age bracket, nearly one-third (31 percent) are in the thirty to sixty-four age group, while one-fourth (twenty-three percent) are age sixty-five and over. There are three women for every two men in this single-adult group. The cities with very large numbers of single adults are Boston (53 percent of its adults are not married now), San Francisco and Washington, D.C. (where half of the adults are not married), and St. Louis, Cleveland, Chicago, Los Angeles, and New Orleans. These single adults are purchasing more than one-fourth of the condominium units being sold, and an increasing number are moving to suburbia.

The other large group that feels neglected by the churches

is composed of single parents. Many of them feel more than simply neglected; they feel that the people in the churches, with their husband-wife emphasis, reject them. In the nation as a whole there are 1.7 million divorced parents with children living at home, another 2.8 million widows and widowers with children at home, and another 1.9 million one-parent families where either the husband or wife is absent. Thus there are 6.5 million single-parent homes with children.

If all these groups were distributed on an even basis, it would mean that in the average congregation the adult membership (age eighteen and over) would resemble this distribution:

- 44 percent husbands and wives living together with children at home
- 40 percent husbands and wives living together with no children under eighteen years of age at home
- 6 percent single adults who have never married
- 4 percent widows and widowers living alone
- 5 percent one-parent households with children at home
- 2 percent other persons not included in the above categories
- 100 percent

How does this compare with the distribution of the adult membership of your congregation? To which group is your congregation primarily oriented? Which group is largely neglected—or rejected—by most of the congregations in your community? How many mature or "career" bachelors in your congregation were not reared in your community? How hard is it for a new single-adult member to become a part of the "fellowship circle"? Is there any congregation in your community undertaking a specialized ministry to one-parent families? To divorced parents with children at home? Do the responses to these questions suggest areas your congregation should consider as it looks at its responsibilities in evangelism and membership recruitment?

Seven Characteristics of Growing Churches

The previous discussion has been focused largely on the potential new members of the churches in the coming years. It may also be helpful to review a few of the characteristics of the churches which have shown the most consistent record of growth during the early years of the 1970s. As we look at the congregations with a consistent record of growth, seven characteristics keep reappearing. Not every growing church reflects every one of these characteristics, but most of them are present in nearly every growing congregation.

The first, the most highly visible, and the most important of these seven characteristics is a strong emphasis on biblical preaching. People today are hungry for biblical preaching. While the bottom has fallen out of the market for ordinary, topical preaching, the market demand for excellent biblical preaching has never been stronger than it is today, in the second half of the 1970s.

Second, the growing congregation of today and tomorrow has an active evangelistic emphasis which is more than an attitude and more than rhetoric. It has its most important expression in lay persons who have a faith to share, a burning desire to share it, an ability to articulate that faith in witnessing to others, a firm conviction that the church does represent the body of Jesus Christ, a concern for people outside the church, and a willingness to help others make a response to the challenge of the Christian gospel.

In the language that is often used in the foreign mission field, the growing churches of today and tomorrow have a cadre of indigenous lay evangelists. They may be identified as "Fishermen's Clubs" or "Visitation-Evangelism Teams" or WIN groups, or perhaps simply as an evangelism committee; but for all practical purposes they can be described as volunteer lay evangelists who are indigenous to the culture, social class, and region served by the congregation.

Third, many congregations can be described in terms of two circles. The larger, outer circle represents the membership of the congregation. The smaller—and sometimes much smaller—inner circle represents the fellowship group. Frequently people are welcomed into the membership circle, but are not allowed into the fellowship circle until after they have served an informal, indefinite, and undefined, but very real, "probationary period." This may run from a few months in some groups to several years in others. Many new members move away or "drop out" before they ever complete this probationary period and thus are never admitted into the fellowship circle.

In the growing churches of today and tomorrow the fellowship circle is at least as large as the membership circle, and usually larger. Historically one of the best examples of this has been, and in some congregations still is, the adult Sunday school class. Adult newcomers are welcomed into the warm, supportive, and nurturing fellowship of the Christian community by way of an adult Sunday school and subsequently unite with that congregation. They are assimilated into the fellowship even before they become members!

Another example of how this fellowship circle may be larger than the membership circle can be found in the circles and other small groups in the women's organization of the local church. Here again people are often received into the fellowship before formally becoming members of the congregation.

Closely related to this is a fourth characteristic of the growing church of today and tomorrow, namely, the capability to assimilate new members into the fellowship, life, program, and ministry of the church. To be more specific, this means that the leaders affirm the idea that one of the reasons for the existence of the Christian church is to provide opportunities for people to express their commitment to Jesus Christ as Lord and Savior through the church. Christian commitment includes the opportunity for people to respond to the love of God as expressed in and through Jesus Christ. The growing church recognizes that different people have different gifts and different needs, and so it

151

intentionally presents a wide variety of opportunities for members to affirm and respond to their commitment through the church. The growing church seeks unity, not in conformity, but in Christ.

This is a more controversial point than it may at first appear. Several of the most respected contemporary authorities on evangelism and church growth contend that the only way for a congregation to grow is to focus on a very narrow slice of the population spectrum. Some of these authorities argue that the congregations most likely to grow are those which are homogeneous in terms of the cultural, educational, racial, theological, economic, and vocational characteristics of the members. There is considerable truth to this argument. Homogeneous congregations usually find it easier to reach and assimilate people who are outside the life of any church than do heterogeneous congregations. The major exception to that generalization is the *intentionally pluralistic* congregation, which carefully and systematically develops the group life of the congregation (see pages 192-93) and sees itself not as a congregation of people, but rather as a congregation of congregations, groups, and individuals.

Though it runs counter to a basic assumption of many church leaders, a fifth characteristic of the growing church of today and tomorrow is that it does not "raise its own members." It is not a congregation filled with adults who are the children and grandchildren of older members. Frequently that is a description of the declining church of today and tomorrow! In today's growing church most of the adults are first-generation members of the congregation. They did not grow up in the Sunday school of that particular congregation. Between 75 and 100 percent of the adult members of today's growing church united with that congregation after they had passed their eighteenth birthday.

In the typical growing church of today and tomorrow less than one-fourth of the high school seniors of ten years ago are active members of the congregation today. The growing church accepts the fact that its youth ministry is preparing people for membership in some other congregation when these youth of today become the adults of tomorrow.

A sixth characteristic of the growing church of today and tomorrow is that in addition to the traditional "package" of program and ministries which can be found in nearly every congregation, it has one or more specialties in ministry. These specialties range from excellence in music to a day care center, a bus ministry, Sunday school classes for retarded persons, a ministry to one-parent families, a counseling center, a special ministry to single young adults, a handbell choir, or a special effort to help senior citizens express their commitment in ministry to others.

Regardless of the nature or content of this specialty in ministry, in the growing churches it has five common characteristics. (a) It is person-centered; (b) it intentionally includes an evangelistic dimension; (c) it provides opportunities for members to be directly and personally involved in ministry to people outside the church; (d) it offers opportunities for members to express themselves through use of their creative skills (by contrast much of what is asked of volunteers in the rest of the church program places a comparatively high premium on competence in verbal skills); and (e) it helps clarify the identity, role, and self-image of the particular church to both members and non-members throughout the community.

Finally, the growing church of today and tomorrow has a minister who likes people, is concerned about and responsive to their spiritual needs, and is happy in his work as a pastor. When asked about today and tomorrow, he cannot think of anything he would rather do than be the pastor of a church, or any church he would rather serve than the one he is now serving.

As thousands of Christian congregations in the United States enter into a new era of church growth, these are seven of the characteristics which keep reappearing in church after church.

VIII How Much Should We Pay Our Minister?

The senior minister at the thousand-member Old First Church, who came there in 1955 after nine years in two other congregations, is paid a cash salary of $13,600 for 1975. His associate, in his fifth year out of seminary, receives a cash salary of $10,000 for 1975. Both receive similar "fringe benefits" (which aren't "fringe" anymore— they're part of the basic "package") in terms of housing, utilities, health insurance, pension, car allowance, and two weeks leave annually for conferences and for continuing education. The major difference in these benefits is three weeks vacation a year for the associate minister and four weeks for the senior minister (he is a workaholic, however, and never takes more than two weeks a year).

When the finance committee met to discuss salaries for 1976, Harry Jones suggested, "Considering the impact of inflation, I believe anything less than a 9 percent increase would be a rank injustice." "I agree," commented Jack Russell, "but the big impact of inflation has been on food, and since both ministers have children at home, I move that we recommend a $1,200 increase for each one. That's approximately 9 percent for our senior minister, and since each will receive the same amount, I don't believe anyone can object to that." The motion carried without a dissenting vote. What do you think of that decision?

The minister at the 165-member Oak Grove Church has

announced that he plans to retire on December 31. He is a seminary graduate and has been serving that rural congregation on a full-time basis since 1955; but he is now sixty-nine years old, and he and his wife want to spend their remaining years in the sun in Arizona. Their only child, who is now in his middle forties, lives in Phoenix. For 1975 Oak Grove paid a cash salary of $6,000 plus $1,200 housing allowance, full pension payments, and $600 for car allowance. Recognizing the impact of inflation, they decided on an increase of nearly 12 percent to $6,700 for 1976. What do you think of that decision?

At Bethany Church the members of the finance committee discuss the pastor's salary for 1976 and one question is asked repeatedly: "What is fair?" In setting the 1975 salary the members of this 600-member congregation in a city of 25,000 residents had tried to be fair. They had increased the cash salary to $12,600, which was exactly 50 percent above the 1968 salary and thus had "kept up" with the increase in personal income for the population of the nation as a whole. In 1971 they had remodeled the parsonage at a cost of $4,700, and in 1972 they had extended the pastor's vacation to three full weeks. After long discussion they decided to increase the 1976 salary by slightly over 10 percent to $13,900, to extend the pastor's vacation to four weeks, and to increase the car allowance from $1,000 to $1,200. In order to fit this into a $59,000 budget for 1976, they hold the figure for benevolences at $10,800, the same as for 1974 and 1975, and reduce the figure for maintenance of the sixty-three-year-old church building from $2,800 for 1975 to $1,800 for 1976. What do you think of this decision?

Unintentional Messages

At Old First Church the decision included these implications: (a) an increase of 12 percent for the associate minister and slightly over 9 percent for the senior minister, and (b) the reinforcement of a pattern which suggests that the difference in experience and responsibilities between the two ministers is worth only $150 per year of experience. The senior minister received a message, *which had not been sent intentionally*, which he read as saying "(a) The finance committee believes that the associate minister increased his competence as much in this past year as it took you eight years to do at his age; and (b) we are more favorably impressed by the accomplishments of the associate minister during the past twelve months than we are with what you have accomplished during the same period, so we are narrowing the differential in salaries."

At Oak Grove the net effect of the decision will be a change to some other arrangement for providing ministerial leadership when the present pastor retires at the end of the year. The combination of cash salary, housing allowance, and car allowance for a 1975 graduate ranges between $11,000 and $13,000—or $2,500 to $4,500 more than the congregation presently feels it can afford to pay. Inflation is forcing this congregation to go from a full-time pastor to a part-time minister.

At Bethany the choices included (a) a minimum salary increase for the minister, (b) seeking a 15 percent increase in total receipts for 1976 in order to both "keep up" with the general increases in salaries and also increase benevolence giving, and (c) a moderate salary increase for the minister "paid for" out of benevolence giving and by deferring certain building maintenance items. Though the second alternative might have been the wisest course of action, the finance committee chose the third alternative.

"How much has the cost-of-living index gone up in the past year?" "What are other churches of comparable size doing?" "How much did we raise it last year?" Questions such as these tend to dominate the conversation as laymen in the local church gather to set the pastor's compensation for the coming year. These are very important questions, and each one tends to influence the final decision. Unfortunately, however, they tend to divert attention from several other factors which deserve far more consideration than they have been receiving. Five have been singled out for attention here.

"What Do You Mean, Compression?"

Perhaps the most subtle of these five factors is what personnel directors in private and public agencies refer to as "compression." In most organizations there is some financial reward for experience. Typically, the person with technical or professional skills and with five or ten or fifteen years experience receives $1,000 to $5,000 a year more than the individual in a similar position who is fresh out of school. When the entrance salaries in a profession increase at a rapid rate, there is a tendency for this gap to be reduced. During the teacher shortage of the 1960s, this produced a serious morale problem. It was not unusual for a teacher graduating in 1975 to start at a higher salary in school system A than was being paid to a teacher in school system B who had graduated from the same university five years earlier. The same situation prevails today with librarians, police officers, and social workers. As the entrance salaries rise more rapidly than the annual increments paid for experience, the salary scale is compressed.

The same compression pattern can be seen in the compensation paid clergymen. It is not unusual for a seminary graduate to be offered a cash salary of $7,600 to $8,000 a year, plus $600 for utilities, plus $1,200 car allowance, plus pension, health and life insurance, and housing. It is also not unusual to find ministers who graduated from seminary ten or fifteen years ago who look at this compensation package and exclaim, "That's not only a lot more than I received when I started, it's more than I am receiving now!"

Up or Out

A closely related issue can best be described by an analogy. Officers in the armed forces are familiar with the phrase "up or out." It means that after an officer reaches a specified age (which varies with rank) and has spent a certain number of years in the same rank, he is either promoted or retired. The reason for this is relatively simple. There are more openings in the table of organization for majors than for colonels, and there are more openings for colonels than for brigadier generals. Those who do not get promoted get out.

A similar pattern can be seen in the pastorate today. There are many more congregations paying a cash salary of $6,000 to $12,000 a year than there are congregations paying $12,000 to $18,000. As the years roll by and a pastor acquires greater experience and more family obligations, he may expect to move up out of the $6,000 to $12,000 salary range into a higher income bracket. In recent years the number of ministers who have the desire, experience, and *competence* to move into pastorates paying $12,000 a year or more has been increasing at a much faster pace than the number of vacancies resulting from retirements, deaths, and other changes. There are many reasons for this, but one is the relatively small number of ministers retiring each year. This is a result of the combination of the small number of men entering the ministry in the 1928–1941 period and the relatively large number of seminary graduates in the 1951–1965 period. Many from this last group of ministers now have the experience to move into the top salary churches—but the vacancies are not there, since the shortage of older ministers means that many of these pulpits are now filled with pastors who are fifteen or twenty years from retirement.

The result is a drastic limit on vocational mobility within the ministry. The forty- to fifty-year-old pastor in the $8,000 to $12,000 salary range with fifteen or twenty years of experience who wants to move finds himself with a very limited range of choices unless he is willing to take a reduction in compensation.

A significant number of these men, on finding they cannot move up, are deciding to move out of the ministry into secular employment. While most of these decisions to leave the ministry are made for a complex set of reasons, of which salary is of varying importance, it is a significant factor for many ministers, especially those who have two or three children of college age.

This situation is complicated by two additional considerations. The first is the tendency for many of the larger congregations to seek a pastor who is under forty-five years of age. This means that many ministers who were patiently looking forward to serving a larger congregation suddenly discover that opportunity has passed them by. Today the man of forty-eight is considered too young to be President of the United States or to serve in the Cabinet, and too old to be called as pastor of First Church.

The other complication is that for a quarter of a century the vocational mobility for ministers was increasing as a result of the creation of hundreds of positions in denominational and interdenominational agencies and various forms of specialized ministries—campus ministry, new church development, college teaching, the foreign mission field, community organization, and other positions outside the parish. Today not only is the number of these positions not increasing, in several denominations the number is being drastically reduced.

The net result is that the pressures for "up or out" are being directed more to the option of "out" because of the narrowing of the "up" channel.

"But That Isn't Fair!"

"Are you trying to tell me that we are going to have to raise the salary we pay by $1,500 if we want to find a man of Dr. Brown's competence and experience?" asked the chairman of the pastor search committee at Main Street Church. He was asking this question of the denominational executive in charge of pastoral placement. Four months earlier, Dr. Brown had announced his retirement plans, and now, with the actual day of his retirement only five weeks away, the committee was beginning to feel the pressure. Their first step after organization had been to ask the regional executive in charge of placement to meet with them, and they had reached the point where they were discussing salary.

"Let me be more precise," replied the denominational executive. "I am saying you should be prepared to pay at *least* $1,500 more than you are now paying if you want to attract the type of minister you are describing. You're now paying Dr. Brown a cash salary of $10,500 plus $600 travel allowance. If you move that up to $12,000 plus $1,000 travel, I think it will greatly increase the number of ministers who might be interested and who meet your specifications. If you raise it to $11,000 for salary plus $1,000 travel, I expect you will find yourself with a very short list to choose from."

"But that isn't fair!" exclaimed a member of the committee. "If we raise the salary $1,000 or $2,000 right after Dr. Brown retires after serving this congregation for seventeen years, what will people think?"

"I'll tell you what some of us will think," responded another member of the committee. "Some of us will think it's a slap in Dr. Brown's face. People will think that we didn't appreciate him and deliberately waited until he retired before raising the salary to the level this church should be paying in today's world."

This is a common dilemma for a congregation to find itself in when the minister, who has served as their pastor for ten or fifteen or more years, retires, dies, or moves. More often than not, when that congregation goes into the ministerial marketplace to seek a replacement, it finds the salary it has been paying is $500 to $3,000 below the level being paid by similar congregations in similar circumstances. If it does not raise the salary substantially, it has a short list of qualified ministers to choose from, but if it does boost the salary substantially, this action can be construed by people as a negative reflection on the minister who served so long.

Shortage or Surplus of Ministers?

For years the churches in American Protestantism have been faced with a shortage of pastors. The decline in seminary enrollment resulting from the low birthrate of the 1930s, the growing demand for ministers in nonparish positions during the 1950s and 1960s, the boom in new church development in the 1950–1966 period, combined with the normal loss due to deaths, retirements, and men leaving the professional ministry, produced a situation in which many congregations found it took a year or two to fill a pastorate vacancy.

In recent years this has changed sharply. The shift first became apparent in the Episcopal Church, followed by the United Presbyterian Church, the Presbyterian Church U.S., and the American Lutheran Church. It is now occurring within the Lutheran Church in America, The United Methodist Church, and other denominations. The most obvious manifestation of the shift is that in many states the pastor who has been serving his present parish for five or six or seven years and is ready to move finds that the choices open to him are discouragingly few.

On the other hand a great many laymen and a significant number of denominational officials are still insisting that there is a shortage of ministers.

What is the actual situation? Is there really a shortage or a surplus?

In response to this question two comments are in order.

First, in every profession—and the ministry is no exception —there is always a shortage of the unusually talented and capable individuals and a surplus of persons who are difficult to place.

Second, and of far greater importance, is the impact of salary changes on the market. As was pointed out earlier, one of the changes has been that, on a percentage basis, starting salaries for seminary graduates have increased more rapidly than have salaries for experienced ministers. One result is the "compression" of the salary scale described earlier. Another is that the salaries for seminary graduates have increased at a faster rate than the capability and/or willingness of many congregations to increase the amount they pay. As a result, the congregation that has had a seminary-trained minister for the past twenty years and now has a vacant pulpit may find itself priced out of the market. In specific terms, literally hundreds of parishes that paid their last minister, who held a seminary degree, a cash salary that ranged between $6,000 and $7,000 (the exact figure varies across the nation and by denomination) now finds itself with a vacant pulpit and no seminary graduates on the list of possible new ministers.

The natural reaction of the members of these congregations is to think that there must be a shortage of ministers.

On the other hand, the seminary graduate who expects a beginning salary in the $7,000 to $8,500 range is disillusioned to discover that he has very few alternatives open to him as he prepares to enter the professional ministry. What happened to that great shortage of ministers he was always hearing about when he entered seminary?

A more precise statement of this situation would be: While there is a growing surplus of seminary graduates, there is still a shortage of ministers for the congregations that want a full-time seminary trained pastor but cannot pay the starting salary expected by today's seminary graduates. Or, as one Presbyterian staff person responsible for pastoral placement said, "We have a huge surplus of ministers for the

$15,000 pulpits, and a serious shortage of men for the $6,000 and $7,000 pulpits."

Inflation and Social Security

Perhaps the least visible of these five neglected aspects of the salary discussion is a result of the combination of inflation and the changing federal legislation on Social Security.

Until recently a minister could choose either to be covered by Social Security or to remain outside the system. Now the law has been changed, and every clergyman must be covered unless prevented by religious scruples. Unlike lay employees of the churches, clergymen are defined as "self-employed" and pay one and one-half times the rate paid by other employees, while the employer does not pay anything. The combination of inflation and the growing political strength of the elderly has caused the Congress to sharply increase the benefits paid, with a resulting increase in the tax.

The impact of these trends can be seen by looking at a specific example. In 1965, one minister received a salary of $6,600 and paid a self-employed Social Security tax of $259.20. For 1975, his salary has jumped all the way up to $13,200—a very impressive increase of $6,600 in ten years. The fact that his cash salary doubled in ten years is not as impressive as it first appears, however. Inflation canceled out over $5,200 of that increase. The buying power of this pastor's $13,200 in the marketplace of 1975 is equivalent to the buying power of $8,000 back in 1965. What appeared to be a $6,600 increase over a ten-year period has shrunk to approximately $1,400 after discounting the impact of inflation.

In addition, however, this pastor's self-employed Social Security tax will be $1,043 under the latest revision in Social Security payments and taxes. This is an increase of

$783 a year or $65 a month over what he paid in 1965. Thus, the combined effect of inflation and the increase in Social Security taxes has wiped out $6,000 of what appeared to be a $6,600 increase in his cash income. Since his federal and state income taxes increased by approximately $800 in this ten-year period, his real purchasing power after taxes has actually decreased by $200 a year, or approximately $16 a month!

These five factors are among those most often neglected when the pastor's compensation is being discussed. Giving more attention to them may be one avenue for improving pastor-parish relationships.

What's a Church to Do?

As difficult as it is to deal adequately and rightly with staff compensation, churches need a lot of guidance on how they might begin to measure up. There are several significant possibilities that churches are finding useful.

First, get the responsibility for recommendations regarding compensation into the hands of a group of church leaders who can give church staff personnel the kind of help they need to do the job. For many churches this will mean establishing a regular church committee on personnel as a perennial committee. Such a committee would have primary responsibility for recommending a staff compensation plan, as well as other personnel activities, for example, preparing written job descriptions for all church staff positions, assisting in employment procedures, helping to evaluate performance of staffers, and recommending compensation adjustments.

Not to have a group giving attention to personnel matters in a comprehensive manner is one way to assure that deficiencies and inequities will continue. The regular budget-planners simply cannot take the time needed to keep up with personnel details, any more than they can keep up with all matters related to church properties, church education ministries, and the myriad other details which are part of the total operation of a church. What they *can* do is to focus on anticipating sources of income; appropriately receiving, handling, accounting for, and reporting on the expenditure of funds; recommending budget allocations requested by various groups in the church, after necessary modification of these requests in consultation with the requesting groups; and giving guidance in other financial matters in the life of the church. To put it another way, the regular financial planning groups in a church have enough to do without the added responsibility for personnel evaluation and compensation. Develop some personnel specialists in your church to do personnel-related work!

Second, let the personnel committee develop and help administer a formalized staff compensation plan that includes the pastor and all other compensated staff workers. Robertsville Church did this very thing, and the work was done entirely by a committee of laymen. The pastor led in getting the committee appointed and approved, and served as a resource person regarding requests for information.

This committee determined to relate their compensation plan to the community in which they lived. They researched such factors as average family income, effective buying income per household, and the distribution of cash income for various income brackets in the community.

The committee conducted their own survey of churches of comparable size and situation. In addition, they acquired data from surveys other churches had made, as well as from compensation studies provided by the denominational research department.

Significantly, the committee researched the compensation of the professional personnel categories which were dominant in their city. They concluded that a professional person could double his income from the time he graduates from college until he reaches his peak, usually over a twenty-five-year

165

period. On this premise they scheduled the total compensation for their pastor to double from the time of the completion of his first seminary degree to the completion of twenty-five years in the ministry. They planned for the same doubling for the other ministry leaders on the staff, based upon a 25 percent differential between the position of the pastor and that of the next lowest level at a given point in years of service. (Some people suggest a 30 percent differential between levels, while others feel 10 percent is enough.) The schedule for the nonprofessional staff members was based on increasing their salary one and one-half times in fifteen years.

Robertsville Church's schedule projected for their ministers for twenty-five years, and provided for consideration of both years of service and the fluctuations of the Consumer Price Index. Years of service referred to the years elapsing since the minister obtained his first seminary degree or the equivalent. Thus, a pastor coming directly from the seminary to be their pastor would begin at zero years on their schedule, while one who had served for five years in another pastorate would begin with five years' standing on their scale. They provided for all schedules to be adjusted up or down annually by the percentage change in the U.S. Bureau of Labor Statistics Consumer Price Index in comparison with the preceding year. The Consumer Price Index is published weekly in the Business and Finance section of the Sunday *New York Times* in a compilation of economic indicators. The indices for the current month and for the same month in the preceding year are given.

Some church personnel committees individualize their compensation plan to relate compensation increases to the "employment anniversary" of the staff member, in contrast to the small inequity that occurs when salary increases for all become effective the first of each fiscal year. This kind of individual consideration of the staff worker requires a bit more precision in budget-planning and in supervision of the staff members. It is generally tied in with a salary review interview between the supervisor and the supervisee, with recommendation from the supervisor as to whether or not to increase the worker's compensation as budgeted. The evaluation would be based upon the degree of achievement by the supervisee of previously agreed upon measurable goals; and the supervisee's personal development plan for the ensuing year would grow out of the evaluation of how well he achieved the goals of his job. Individualizing the compensation plan to relate to the "employment anniversary" of the staff member heightens the anticipation of the anniversary occasion, and can prove a very helpful stimulus to productivity and to the development of the worker on the job.

A comprehensive compensation plan involves many other decisions. Standard benefit areas in which a personnel committee should recommend policy include vacations, holidays, gifts (seasonal and anniversary), hospital and medical insurance, life insurance, disability insurance, retirement plan, paid moving expenses, housing, car allowance, study leave, book allowance, outside invitations involving time away, etc. A committee on personnel that studies the benefits situation, decides what to include and to upgrade, analyzes the cost of each priced benefit, secures appropriate approval of the proposed benefits, communicates the benefits to staff members, advises and/or supervises in the administration of the plan, and periodically reviews the plan, has a year-round responsibility. Small wonder a church finance committee can't see about all these things and at the same time do its work in the church finance areas!

Third, and in addition to other guidelines to be considered in determining the staff compensation, plan (*a*) to pay as much as you can for the particular job to be performed without (*b*) hurting the worker with the constituency or (*c*) creating a "compression" or an "up or out" situation. (Each of these was discussed earlier in this chapter.) It is wholesome and good for a church to pay what it is able to pay in the light of the services to be rendered. Something is missing in the pastor search committee or the personnel committee that asks, "What will you come for?" or, "What will you have to have in order to come to our church as minister of education?" A fitting question in response, but one that is rarely asked, would be "What can you pay?" Some committees, when seeking references to possible prospects, state something like, "We could go as high at $14,500 if we had to." If they can go that high, perhaps they should deal on that level to begin with. Wouldn't you hate to learn, after you had settled for $12,000, that they would have gone to $14,500? Chances are that all parties think less of the staffer who didn't get the top dollar available, including the staffer himself.

On the other hand, it is possible to "hurt" the worker in some instances by paying too much. He can be hurt in that many of the congregation have misgivings about his compensation if it is considerably out of line with their own. An old rule of thumb suggests that the minister receive compensation equal to the average salary of the heads of the household of the top ten or twenty salaried families in the congregation. Certainly there are other factors to consider, but in many communities this would be a fair guide. No minister wants to be out of reach economically from the majority of his congregation. Churches with an extremely large number of persons on their staff, and with several levels even on their professional staff, have the added hazard of self-contained "compression" within their own staff. To avoid this "compression," and to avoid having those on the lower levels suffer because their salaries are too low, these churches should consider having smaller differentials between levels on their staff organization chart—like 5 or 10 percent. Another alternative is to put the top staffers higher than regular guidelines would suggest, at the risk of creating the gap most churches wish to avoid between the staffer and the constituency. It must be said that more churches are likely to "hurt" their staffers paying too little than by paying too much. The hope, to be sure, is to avoid the "hurt" of either kind.

Fourth, a church should keep its compensation plan current. Many churches learn what current means only when they go to search for a replacement for a good staff member who has moved, and who just might not have moved had they shown adequate interest in keeping current on the compensation. There are many factors, surely, that enter into the moving of a minister—and the current status of the compensation is only one of them. It is seldom the primary factor, but often it is a significant factor. Someone who is in the ministry for the money probably isn't worth his salary, however low it may be. But one certain way a church can convey genuine appreciation to its staff members is by being sensitive in constructive ways to the ebb and flow of the compensation situation.

For example, an annual update of the salaries in the light of the changes in the Consumer Price Index is almost imperative, unless you actually intend to cut a worker's pay. And a 3 to 6 percent merit raise related to job performance, in addition to the cost-of-living increase, is the practice of some progressive churches in which careful study has been done by the committee on personnel. These and other changes, for example in insurance and hospital-medical protection, require almost constant attention in order to keep from falling behind.

What about a church that is too far behind to catch up in a given year? Some churches have been known to give up on the idea of trying to catch up when they discover how far behind they are! A more appropriate approach would be to set some goals over a more reasonable time span, like a three-year period, within which time you will bring the compensation plan up to where it should be at that point. Still another alternative would be to put forth the special effort needed to increase the receipts in order to do what is needed sooner than over a three-year period.

Before coins and currency were so common, in the days

of the Roman legions, there were times when a soldier received his pay in the form of salt. Our word "salary" comes from the same Latin source as our word "salt." Hence the expression "worth his salt." A minister—a worker on a church staff—should be worth his salt. A church, of all institutions, should deal fairly with its workers who are worth their salt. A thoughtful compensation plan that is kept current and that is equitably administered will go a long way toward solving many of the problems facing the churches and their ministers in these times.

IX Financing Capital Improvements

"First we shape our buildings and then our buildings shape us." This frequently quoted statement by Winston Churchill highlights several of the very crucial issues facing anyone concerned with creative church administration. One of the most common is that the size and design of the meeting place controls both the schedule and much of the content for worship and education in many congregations.

Two of these issues, in which emotion is frequently more influential than reflection, are the financing of capital improvements and the use of the building. Before moving on to discuss the role of the worshiping congregation as a landlord, it may be helpful to look first at the importance and the financing of the meeting place.

A church needs an identifiable base in which to assemble and from which to operate. Early churches met wherever they could. Often they met in the homes of members. This home-church approach still offers for some people an atmosphere conducive to intimate corporate worship, good fellowship, and concern for outreach. But few homes are adequate for carrying out the functions of a church building for an extended time. Meaningful worship experiences, good fellowship, and concern for outreach to bring others into these and other joyous benefits, most likely portend the provision of more capital improvements, and sooner rather than later. This lesson has been learned repeatedly by inner

171

city congregations which began in a storefront and found they needed larger and more adequate physical facilities.[1]

On the other hand, congregational leaders can over-emphasize buildings. They can go too far into debt. The members' concern can be drawn to oppressive financial obligations to such an extent that they cannot give primary concern to the priority business of the church—to bring persons to God through Christ, with all the quantitative and qualitative factors which this priority includes. To over-extend a church's finances is to risk chilling members' enthusiasm and thus to make the church become a poor witness to the world. For different reasons, shoddy buildings can have the same effect.

The building can set the pattern for ministries. People are seldom reached for whom space is not provided. A church can build reasonably well-constructed buildings and fund them, and also fund other significant ministries within and without the home base. Despite the rhetoric on the subject, church construction has never exceeded more than ten dollars per year per church member in the United States. We are able to do what we must do to fund the buildings we need.

Before a church considers its options for funding buildings the members should look very carefully at their present facilities and their use. If this is not done, it becomes very easy to fall victim to the edifice complex, in which buildings are built as monuments to energetic leadership. Questions like "To what extent are our present buildings being used?" and "What could we economically do with our present buildings to make them suit the needs?" and "What would we actually do in a new or renovated building which we could not do fairly easily in an existing building which is or could be made available?" should be asked and thoroughly answered in detail. Often some well-timed consultation by

---

[1] For an elaboration of this point see Lyle E. Schaller, *Planning for Protestantism in Urban America* (Nashville: Abingdon Press, 1965), pp. 167-71.

a professionally competent person can help your members determine whether or not they need major capital improvements. A committee of members can lead the church in the study. Then if the need warrants it, you can proceed to determine just what you will need. If the need does not warrant more major outlay for buildings, you can turn your attention back to those priority concerns like funding new or improved ministries, more adequately compensating persons who lead in the ministries and the mission causes you espouse.

How Do Churches Find Money for Building?

One simple answer to the question of how churches get money for building seems not to appear frequently enough: churches get money for building from their members. Regardless of the approach they use to get access to money for paying the immediate bills for construction and related costs, sooner or later the money comes from the gifts of members, supplemented to a limited extent by persons outside the membership. By and large, the members pay.

Members pay back the money which is borrowed from conventional lending agencies such as banks and insurance companies. Members pay back the principal amount borrowed. Members pay back the interest on the principal. Some churches and a few entire denominations presently pay more interest annually on church building debts than they give for all causes beyond the local congregation.

The most common type of loan churches use for capital improvements is a secured long-term loan, with the church property assigned to the lender as collateral. The term of the loan may extend from five years to fifteen or twenty. Fifteen years is the anticipated term of most of these loans, though their average actual life is approximately eight years, owing to a variety of factors ranging from early payoff to refunding (a nicer way to say refinancing). A conventional loan for fifteen years, negotiated at 1974 prime interest rates, would call for an amount equal to 1.8 to 2 times the amount borrowed to be paid back over the fifteen-year period. For example, $100,000 borrowed would be repaid by $180,000 to $200,000.

There are advantages to borrowing from conventional lending agencies to fund capital improvements. One of the most obvious advantages is that the money can be available immediately upon the completion of the necessary negotiations and approvals. You can enjoy the benefits of early possession and use of the property. In some instances this factor alone makes borrowing the most attractive approach. Another advantage may be the extended time allowed for repaying the amount borrowed, this time occasionally being as long as twenty years. This latter advantage might be removed in times of fluctuating interest rates, with lenders preferring shorter periods for repayment, or, as an alternative, requiring interest rates to escalate or de-escalate with the market, causing amounts of payments to vary with rising or falling interest rates.

There are some critical points regarding borrowing which church leaders should observe. One imperative is for the church to be certain that it is registered with the appropriate state office (the secretary of state, or the attorney general, in most states) as a corporation. Such registration makes clear for all legal purposes the fact that the church is an entity, a body, and not just a random roster of individuals, any one of whom may deal or be dealt with as the church. A competent attorney can guide you in becoming incorporated. *American Jurisprudence Legal Forms Annotated* can supply sample incorporation procedures and forms. Most lending agencies would require evidence of incorporation as part of the approval process.

Another critical point related to borrowing is to determine the limits of your ability to repay, and stay within those limits. The limits vary from church to church, because conditions of churches differ. Certain limits might be wise for

174

one church, but unsafe for another. One church might be able to commit 35 to 40 percent of its annual receipts for capital debt repayment and still not hamper its missions and ministries efforts. Another church might be courting trouble to commit as much as 30 percent for capital debt repayment. Church members' harmony, the obvious nature of the need for capital improvements, the confidence of members in their leaders, church growth history and prospects, and the general state of the economy are among the factors to consider in determining the limits of your ability to repay. Also it is wiser as a rule to set up the repayment rate at a level amount throughout the repayment timetable than to begin with lower payments and then raise the amount of repayments at some point in time when you think you will have more members to help with the obligation. Strenuous debt repayment schedules have a way of not attracting new members to the membership and also of getting members' attention off the necessary priority of outreach and onto the financial concerns, to the possible detriment of both causes.

Members also pay back the money acquired by the sale of church bonds. The bond approach is a form of borrowing whereby a church borrows from members, friends, and general investors, and issues to each investor the church's bond assuring repayment of the amount borrowed plus a fixed rate of interest. As in the area of conventional lending, there are competent professional firms whose services a church might employ to provide a wide range of services related to financing capital improvements by means of bonds. It is vital to have adequate guidance on the complex approach which bonds involve.

Most of the advantages and critical points to observe regarding borrowing that were mentioned above in the comments on conventional loans are also pertinent to the bond approach. One of the unique aspects of bonds is that, in many instances, the members are actually lending themselves the money, and repaying themselves both the principal and the interest, plus the costs of servicing the issue. Some members even borrow from a conventional lender and buy their church's bonds, in order eventually to effect a personal savings for some future family need or interest.

There are variations of these two basic approaches, the conventional loan or the church bond, which churches find useful. Often a church might find it necessary to use more than one of these during the same time period in order to obtain the amount needed for their capital improvement financing.

The Cash Pledge Approach

Members give the money for their building needs by still another basic approach, classified as the cash pledge approach. In this method, members are called upon to commit themselves to give an amount they determine, above their regular gifts, and usually over a three-year collection period. Their commitment is a statement of their good-faith intention. It is not a promissory note, but a pledge of what they will commit themselves to do. The pledge may be increased, decreased, or canceled at the discretion of the pledger.

There is nothing to repay in the cash pledge approach. There is no borrowing involved in the basic transaction. There is no repayment of principal. There is no interest payment. Members who pledge simply give what they commit themselves to give, as a sum in addition to their usual gifts. Some will give who don't pledge. The church begins to receive these gifts immediately after the commitments are taken, but the full amount of the pledge is usually received by the end of the three-year collection period.

The most obvious advantage of the cash pledge approach is its low cost. The costs of a campaign can most often be limited to less than 3 percent of the amount pledged. If a church can lead its members to pledge to give $100,000 over a three-year collection period, this easily translates into a cost of less than $3,000. Compare this with the additional cost of $80,000 to $100,000 for a loan made at 1974 rates for a fifteen-year period, and you can readily see why some churches are interested in the cash pledge approach. Couple with this the added fact that, whatever the appproach to acquiring the money, the money must come from the members themselves, and the lower cost approach begins to take on added attractiveness.

There are some disadvantages to the cash pledge approach. Most obvious is the fact that the full amount is not available until the end of the collection period, usually three years hence. Also true is the fact that the amount a church will pledge cannot be precisely determined until the campaign to lead them to pledge is over. Again, some churches cannot get all the funds needed by the cash pledge approach (which may also be true of the borrowing approaches). Yet some do get what they need.

Several hundred churches have used the cash pledge approach in recent years. Generally they have found it to be a very satisfactory way of funding or helping to fund capital improvements. Almost always the regular gifts increase, even though members are giving beyond their regular gifts to the cash pledge effort. Churches usually receive at least 90 percent of the cash pledged by the end of the three-year period, with many going beyond 100 percent. Even if they do not get all they need in cash gifts, what they do get is relatively inexpensive; and it serves as rather convincing evidence of a church's ability to repay, should there be a need for either interim or long-term financing. If borrowing becomes necessary in addition to a cash pledge, further savings can accrue because of the increase in giving from both the regular gifts and the added giving, enabling the church to set up a repayment schedule of shorter duration, with a commensurate saving of interest.

What is the essence of a cash pledge campaign? The idea is quite simple. The congregation must determine the needs for capital improvement (see suggestions about discovering the church and community needs in chapter 6) in consultation with an architect; develop the plans for the capital improvement; inform the members, and interested friends, in detail, of both the needs and the planned improvements intended to enable the church to meet those needs; and provide a discreet and orderly process by which members can commit themselves to give over the three-year collection period. There is a great deal of detail involved in accomplishing these rather simple sounding results, but the idea itself is not complicated.

Organizing the Financial Campaign

Let's look at some of the features of a cash pledge campaign. The campaign idea needs to be thoroughly clear to members in terms of needs, planned improvement, and an above-and-beyond commitment of cash gifts to be collected over the three-year period. Lead the congregation to approve the campaign two to three months before the focal time of conducting the campaign.

Most often you will need the help of a trained consultant to guide you in planning for and implementing a campaign. The cost of engaging a reputable consultant is included in prior statements about the cost of this approach. When the congregation approves the idea of conducting the campaign, let them also authorize the employment of a consultant. Check with your denominational stewardship leaders for suggestions regarding consultants. Some pastors are themselves competent to lead their church in such a campaign; but keep in mind that there is work for a pastor to do as pastor in such a campaign, in addition to the very specialized work of financial consultant, and the regular pastoral responsibilities.

With the help of an existing committee within the church, or with an ad hoc committee, whose members know the church members reasonably well, prepare to present three things to the congregation for approval six to ten weeks before the first Sunday of the focal time: (1) a total goal for the amount to be pledged; (2) a temporary steering committee for the campaign proper; and (3) a focal time of six weeks on the church calendar for the campaign proper (actually six Sundays, with the weeks between).

The members who work on the goal figure to present to the church need to make a careful study of the giving potential of the members, in terms of what the members actually *could* give if they would. Do this discreetly, taking great care to avoid the idea of assessing members for certain amounts. In the light of the total potential for such giving by your members, and in the light of the fact that many will not give what they are capable of giving, and with an ample measure of faith and harmonious spirit, arrive at the goal appropriate for your church. There are some rules of thumb about what a church might do, and they can help in determining the goal. But they are only rules of thumb. Occasionally a church has been known to give all that the giving potential study suggested they were capable of giving. Most often churches will give between 35 and 50 percent of a good giving-potential study. Another rule of thumb which has merit is one and one-half times the previous year's total receipts. All of this is above the regular giving, and there should be no blending, combining, or mixing of the cash pledge money or the campaign with the regular efforts on behalf of the church budget.

Some churches find it helpful to set more than one goal in a cash pledge campaign. The first, lower-level goal represents a really good effort which produces a pledged amount approximating an amount the church would be quite justifiably happy about. A second, higher-level goal represents something of a miraculous result, perhaps like reaching 25 to 35 percent more than the lower-level goal. The big focus generally is on the more easily attainable of the two goals, with the higher goal getting secondary attention in the educational and promotional campaign.

The steering committee selected or nominated by the ad

hoc committee or other committee should consist of church members who will serve to direct the campaign efforts. The steering committee needs a general director (to be helped by the pastor and the consultant) to give direction to the campaign. A promotion director directs the preparation of a good brochure, oversees some informational mailouts and other general publicity, supervises the preparation and teaching of an appropriate Bible lesson via the Sunday school, and sees that suitable testimonials are scheduled and presented. A director of advanced gifts works with the pastor and selected helpers prior to the church banquet to contact those whose gift potential might be considerably larger than most. A canvass director leads in preparing for and conducting a canvassing visit to the home of every church member family to receive their commitment. A banquet director leads in all arrangements and reservations for a spectacular church banquet and a simultaneous children's party for those aged eight or nine and below. A follow-up director leads a group in completing the few remaining calls to those members who for any reason could not be reached in the regular canvass after the focal time has ended, and in the commitment efforts with new members who join the church during the three-year collection period. A competent campaign secretary directs the clerical work required in a successful campaign. A campaign treasurer, who may also be the regular treasurer of the church, should serve with the steering committee to care for the financing of the campaign. Someone is also needed to prepare refreshments for the canvassers when they return for fellowship and reporting during the days or nights of the canvass visits.

A highlight of the effort to inform, inspire, and challenge to commitment the members during the campaign proper is the brochure, sent to each family very early in the campaign. It should portray in words and pictures the whole idea of the campaign in attractive ways. Another major feature is the church banquet. It is best to have the banquet during the fourth week of the focal time. It should be *the* church social occasion of the decade or the generation, during which members are reminded of the church's history, are given a glimpse of what the future can hold for them and their successors, and are challenged and inspired by the pastor to be prepared to receive the canvassers kindly, and to make a sacrificial commitment to the campaign upon their visit. Do no soliciting during the banquet. Absorb the cost of the dinner in the campaign costs.

Announce the amount of the advanced gifts pledges (including steering committee members' commitments) as one of the items during the banquet program. As with almost every enterprise in which a church engages, the pastor and other leaders must be evidently committed to what they are calling on others to support.

On the fifth Sunday afternoon of the focal time send the trained and financially committed canvassers to the members' homes to discreetly receive members' commitments. Canvass each evening following Sunday five until the work is completed to a point of satisfaction, with visiting canvassers reporting at a specified time each evening. On Sunday six, conclude the campaign. Announce the results. Celebrate. Refer remaining calls in homes to the follow-up director. Close the campaign on Sunday six.

Provide regular and convenient ways of collecting the gifts and reporting them. Some churches use special envelopes designed for the cast pledge gifts. Others combine with their regular offering envelopes a method of recording these gifts. Report the cash pledge gifts along with the regular church gifts, to the congregation and to the individual members, at regular intervals.

To include new members who join the church during the collection period of three years, some churches periodically (three or four times a year) have a mini-banquet for them, and present the whole informational package, paving the way for a home visit later when the new members will have an opportunity to make their commitment to the cash pledge effort. The gifts they give help to offset those of members

181

who for some reason may not fulfill their pledge. Other ways of following up with new members might include use of the mail, special visits to the homes to make the informational presentation and to receive the pledge, and other such suitable methods.

Whatever the method of financing capital improvements, the members are the source. They deserve approaches to funding which have dignity, full participation, integrity, respect for the individual, and discretion. The church administrative leader who can discover, design, or otherwise utilize methods of funding which observe these criteria can enjoy benefits like those Jethro promised to Moses when he advised him in the wilderness: You can get the job done that is needed, and you can endure!

Landlord or Pastor?

Three hundred years ago the Christians of New England were careful to refer to the place where the congregation gathered to worship God as "the meeting place." The word "church" was reserved for use in referring to the called-out community of Christians. This distinction has become blurred with the passage of time, and today the word "church" is widely used to refer to the building which has been constructed as the meeting place for a worshiping congregation.

One of the results of this change in the use of words is the apparently increasing number of congregations which have identified their role as providing a building to house the program and/or staff of a variety of neighborhood organizations and community programs. It is not uncommon to hear comments such as these: "Our church has never been so busy as it is now. Nearly every room is used every day!" "Our church is the first place to which groups and organizations in the neighborhood turn when they need help." "We have made the ministry to the neighborhood the first priority for our church."

Each of these comments came from congregations in which only a handful of members still live in the neighborhood in which the congregation's meeting place is located. In each case only the minister and a few members have any direct involvement in any of the neighborhood-oriented programs or activities housed in the building.

183

Is this creative church administration? The answer to that question will be influenced by how you define that word "church"!

How Did This Happen?

There appears to be no question but that one of the significant trends in urban America is that an increasing number of religious congregations are making their buildings available to a lengthening list of programs and activities which are not directly administered by the congregation owning that property. Among the most common examples of this are the churches which permit or encourage the use of their building as the regular meeting place for a Boy Scout troop, or a local unit of Alcoholics Anonymous, or Weight Watchers, or a service club such as Lions, Kiwanis, or Rotary. During the 1960s this trend accelerated sharply when "the war on poverty" facilitated the creation of hundreds of community actions programs, nursery schools, legal aid offices, health clinics, housing centers, community organizations, and language classes for persons for whom English was a second language. Many of these are housed in church buildings.

What is behind this trend? What caused it to emerge?

To be more precise, five trends came together at the same time and place. First, the post–World War II exodus of people from the older residential neighborhoods to new homes in new subdivisions created a role change for thousands of Protestant congregations. These congregations had been founded decades earlier to serve the people living in a clearly defined residential neighborhood. Many were launched by members from "Old First Church Downtown." As members moved out of the downtown area they suggested that a new church be considered for the neighborhood into which they were moving. Sometimes this began as a Sunday school "outpost." One great wave of these was started in the twenty years preceding World War I, and another wave of these neighborhood churches was launched in the 1920s. During the 1950s thousands of these changed from "neighborhood churches" to "ex-neighborhood churches" as many of the members moved away but regularly returned to their old church in the old neighborhood.

The second of the five trends was the influx of new residents into these neighborhoods. Many of the newcomers came from rural America, Puerto Rico, and Mexico. Blacks, Latinos, and Anglos from Appalachia constituted a large part of the "replacement" population as middle- and upper-class whites moved out to newer housing.

The third trend was the growing support for the statement that "a church should serve the people in the neighborhood in which the church building is located." This concept of "Serve Your Neighborhood" had a popular ring to it, but it produced frustrations for many of the leaders of these ex-neighborhood churches. The newcomers, who often came from a different religious culture and social class than the church was accustomed to serving, did not respond to traditional evangelistic overtures. In some cases there was the added barrier of language. Many congregations responded to these conditions by selling their property and establishing a new meeting place close to the new residences of their members. Others closed. Some elected to stay. They stayed for a variety of reasons, including a strong attachment to the particular place, a determination to continue to try to reach the new residents, the conviction that it was "unchristian to flee," a strong commitment by the pastor to an inner-city ministry, encouragement by denominational leaders, the feeling that relocation represented more radical and frightening change than remaining, the hope that urban renewal would turn back the calendar, financial limitations which may have made relocation an economic impossibility, and the determination of a handful of committed lay persons that God had called them to ministry at that place.

The fourth trend can be seen in the ebb and flow of the

tides of social activism in American Protestantism. One of the first waves of this social activism was the Sunday school. The Sunday school was founded by Robert Raikes in England in the 1780s to combat crime and ignorance. In contemporary terminology it was a preventive measure against juvenile delinquency. The first Sunday schools to be founded in America were devoted almost exclusively to teaching the poor to read and write. When the poor began to display less interest, Lyman Beecher and others encouraged the middle- and upper-class families to send their children in order to keep the Sunday school from dying. An even greater expression of Protestant social activism was the anti-slavery movement. Another was the settlement house concept at the turn of the century. A fourth was the drive for prohibition in the years just before and during World War I. A fifth was the push for economic justice of the 1930s. A sixth was the focus on civil rights, social justice, and the war on poverty of the late 1950s and early 1960s. This sixth wave of social activism reinforced the determination that was expressed in the imperative "Every church should serve the people in its neighborhood."

The fifth and perhaps the decisive trend to encourage greater secular use of church buildings was the appropriation of huge sums of public funds to improve the living conditions of low-to-middle- and low-income persons. The availability of these funds encouraged the creation of a wide range of social welfare, educational, self-help, and empowerment programs. Among the many consequences of this huge effort of the middle and late 1960s was a demand for space that greatly exceeded the supply in many neighborhoods and communities. There emerged a demand for space for weekday programs, for office rooms, and for public meeting places. In many cases the users could not pay the regular market rental rates for the space they required. In the face of this demand for space there were hundreds of strategically located church buildings with a tremendous amount of space that was never used from Monday through Saturday.

When these trends converged in the 1960s, the natural result was a sudden increase in the weekday use of church buildings which were being used less and less by the aging and scattered membership. This process was facilitated by the pressure for "relevance," by the frustration felt by the leaders of these churches in their attempts to reach new-comers to the neighborhood through traditional forms of ministry, and by the importance of a comparatively small number of ministers and lay leaders who were increasingly frustrated when the members of their congregations displayed little interest in a more active participation in ministry to others.

More and more congregations commented about their "busy building." Some members spoke with a sense of pride, accomplishment, and relevance. Other members displayed a much less enthusiastic and supportive attitude and expressed their concern about the excessive wear and tear on the property and the rising costs of maintenance.

In many communities it soon became a mark of distinction for a congregation to have a building which was heavily used by various community and neighborhood agencies and by secular voluntary associations. Likewise many of the members of other congregations in all types of communities began to develop a sense of guilt over the fact that many of the rooms in their building were unused 160 to 168 hours every week.

The Evaluation

One of the characteristics of creative church administration is the built-in self-evaluation process which (1) measures performance against purpose, (2) measures costs against benefits, (3) distinguishes between institutional self-glorification and ministry to people, (4) provides a relevant and usable context for planning and decision-making, and (5) produces a continuing corrective impact on the program-planning process within the congregational or denominational family.

How do you evaluate the use of a church to house neighborhood organizations and community-oriented programs?

It is impossible to place a dollar value on the contributions of those congregations which have encouraged the use of their property by a variety of neighborhood, community, public, and semi-public agencies and groups. If this could be calculated in terms of rents it would total millions of dollars. Another benefit was that it helped to create a favorable attitude toward the Christian church among many people who previously were indifferent or hostile in their view of organized religion. Perhaps most important of all, this opening of church buildings to general community uses has enabled congregations to reach some people with the Good News of Jesus Christ whom they otherwise would not have touched.

None of this came without a price, however, and this side of the story has been largely neglected.

The least important cost has been the wear and tear on the property. Far more serious has been the fact that in too many congregations the members moved to the comparatively passive role of landlord and left the active role of ministry to the neighborhood to their pastor. It became easy for the members to justify the existence of the congregation by saying, "We're in mission through our building." Try to find a proof text for that concept! Maintenance of the building, rather than evangelism, became the form of outreach to the community. Instead of being directly involved in ministry to people, the members could rationalize their inactivity by explaining, "We're a servant church; our building is used by sixteen different groups which serve the people of this community." The impatient pastor who became frustrated at his inability to involve his members in ministry in the neighborhood could gain satisfaction from the fact that at least the church building was "in mission" even if that could not be said about his congregation! In addition, this role provided favorable recognition of him by neighborhood residents, and the psychic rewards which accompany that recognition. Another way of describing this is to note that it increased the gap between the pastor and most of his members.

At this point in the process of developing a frame of reference for evaluation purposes it may be helpful to interrupt and introduce two concepts.

The first is not very old, but is largely forgotten today. This is one of the plans for measuring the efficiency of a public school system which emerged in the second decade of this century when "scientific management" was first developing a following in the educational profession. Known as the "Gary Plan" or the "Platoon School," it included the goal that every room in every building should be in use every hour. The simplicity of this concept swept the nation, and by 1929 it was used in 202 city school systems in forty-one states, including such large cities as Akron, Birmingham, Dallas, Detroit, Portland, Seattle, and Tulsa. This system gave administrators and school board members a simple method for measuring the efficiency of a school system. If in our city the rooms in the school buildings are in use 94 percent of the hours of the day and in your city the usage rate is only 81 percent, it is obvious that we have a more efficient school system in our city than you have in your community. During the late 1920s and the 1930s the Gary Plan began to be abandoned as educators placed more emphasis in their evaluation on what was happening to the people in those rooms than on what percentage of the day the room was in use.

The second concept goes back to the use of words and their impact on people's thinking. When someone says the word "landlord," what images come into your mind? What are the words, phrases, and values that come to mind when you think of a landlord? Does the word "landlord" trigger other thoughts and images which are represented by such words and phrases as "buildings," "houses," "things," "complaints," "slumlord," "greed," "avarice," "absentee," "opponent," "rich," "pickets and picket lines," "newspaper headlines," "deteriorating buildings in a deteriorating neighborhood," "substandard," "rent," "money," and "bills"?

Now let's play this same word association game again, but this time using a different word. When someone says the word "pastor," what images come into your mind? Does this word evoke such words and phrases as "friend," "concern," "caring," "unselfish," "Jesus," · "person-centered," "shepherd," "church," "prayer," "minister," "father," "neighbor," and "helpful"?

If we return this discussion to the congregation with its "busy building," it is relevant to note that in many cases this building is the meeting place for a congregation which moved out of the inner city following the close of World War II. A relocated congregation tends to be an alien in a strange land. It brings its own heritage and traditions with it, and rarely are these coterminous with the history and traditions of the community into which it moves. Many of the people, and usually a majority of the leaders, live at least a couple of miles from the new relocation site. For this relocated congregation it is easy to be misled by the illusion that if the building is made available for community activities and programs this will help the church be accepted in the community and thus encourage people to unite with the congregation. The record suggests this is an illusion *unless many of the programs are sponsored, not simply housed, by the congregation and members of the congregation have active leadership roles in most or all of these programs and activities*. Very, very few people join a Christian congregation because they made friends with the building. Most members of any long-established Protestant congregation (*a*) came in because of very strong denominational ties and/or (*b*) knew someone (parent, spouse or future spouse, child, relative, friend, neighbor, fellow employee, etc.) in that congregation before they decided to join. A "busy building" may win "acceptance," but it does not attract new members! The landlord image is far less attractive to people than is the pastoral image of the Christian church.

Perhaps the most critical price tag is that not infrequently the program and ministry of the congregation are seriously inhibited or curtailed because of the decision to maximize use of the building by community and neighborhood groups. The more visible examples of this can be seen where there is a shortage of offstreet parking or where the design of the building prohibits more than two events being held concurrently. The more subtle, less visible, and far more serious expression of this "cost" is in the programs and ministries which are not planned and not implemented by the members, because "someone else has already scheduled the building" for the particular time or occasion. Thus intensive use of the building by community groups and agencies often tends to gradually reduce the program and ministry of the congregation until it is down to a couple of activities on Sunday morning and perhaps one or two during the week. If the congregational leaders use a self-evaluation procedure paralleling the Gary Plan used by public school systems in the first quarter of this century, this will tend to reinforce this trend. The next step often turns out to be dissolution of the congregation.

Perhaps the most subversive cost of this trend is that it may cause the congregation to redefine its sense of purpose, its reason for being, and its self-image. As it drifts into the landlord role this tends to mean a shift away from a direct ministry to people, both members and nonmembers. As was pointed out previously, there is a vast difference between the image associated with the pastoral role of the worshiping community and the image associated with the concept of landlord. Perhaps that is one reason why many of the congregations which emphasize the landlord role tend to minimize the pastoral ministry-to-people role.

XI Five Evaluation Questions

Too often the evaluation process in the church resembles the report card received by the student at the end of the school year. After the report card has been received the student can review it and reflect on the "might have beens" and the wishes that were not turned into reality, but it is too late to do anything more constructive about the past.

A better approach is to ask evaluation questions in a manner which can influence performance and produce creative results. This can be accomplished by a more thoughtful approach to the evaluation process. One of the most important dimensions of creative church administration is that it builds a greater emphasis on quality into the evaluation process, which traditionally has emphasized such quantitative considerations as membership, attendance, and receipts. This can be illustrated by the following five sets of questions, most of which are seldom asked in the typical church.

What Is the Health of the Group Life?

What is the health of the group life in your congregation? How many of the members of your congregation are members of a group which has meaning for them?

If the information were readily available, the most useful group of questions one might ask in seeking to understand the life of the typical church would be these:

1. How many groups are alive and functioning in your congregation in which membership is meaningful to most of the group members?

2. In what year did the persons who find a particular group to be especially meaningful to them join this group? How many of these persons joined during the past five years?

3. What proportion of the members of the congregation are members of one or more of these groups?

4. How many of the adults who joined the congregation during the past five years are members of one of these groups?

A carefully prepared response to this quartet of questions will reveal how "open" the congregation is to newcomers and who the inactive members are, and it will begin to pinpoint the program areas which require improvement. The responses will also identify, by their absence, those program areas which are in serious trouble. A review of the list of members most actively involved in one or more groups will also help identify the people the congregation is able to minister to most effectively.

The larger the congregation, the more important it is to evaluate the quality and health of the group life of the congregation. The above four questions offer a beginning point.

What Is the Median Date?

Closely related to the question of the health of the group life is another question. What is the date which marks the halfway point in the tenure of the present members? Half of the present members joined before that date, and half joined after it. In the typical urban congregation with an average turnover in membership this date is seven to ten years ago.

If that date is less than seven years ago this sparks several other questions. Why are so many people joining the congregation? Can these factors be identified and enhanced? How effective is the assimilation process for these new members?

193

How many of them have been absorbed into the *fellowship* of the congregation? Is the "power group" controlled by people who joined more than seven years ago, or do the newer members have a meaningful voice in the decision-making process? If the newer members have a major voice in the decision-making process, do some of the older former leaders feel neglected? Do they feel they have been passed over? Do they feel that the contributions they made to the congregation in previous years are now going unrecognized? Do these longtime members feel that the present leadership does not appreciate what was done years ago to make today possible and that the advances of yesterday are now being neglected or reversed?

If the date is more than ten years ago, this immediately opens the door to a series of questions on why the congregation is not able to reach more newcomers to the community. Has the "fellowship door" been closed and, if so, when? Who are the leaders? Is there rotation in office?

Who Evaluates Worship?

"Leaders speak only to other leaders" is the old saying used to describe the evaluation and decision-making processes in many organizations. While there is considerable truth in these six words, this is an inadequate descriptive statement of how decisions are made. A more accurate statement would be "Leaders speak only to other leaders, but there is very little evidence to suggest that leaders listen to anyone."

Nowhere does this generalization have greater application than in the planning of the worship experiences in many congregations. The music committee (which frequently consists of one person) plans the music he or she believes is appropriate for corporate worship. The minister preaches the sermons he likes to preach. The ushers play the role which makes them feel comfortable. The hour of the service is scheduled for the convenience of the most articulate members of the governing board. If someone objects or suggests an alternative, the normal and natural reaction is to shift the discussion to what is wrong with the person who is proposing something new.

In some congregations the planning and evaluation of worship is left to the minister. All too often he is dependent on the comments he hears when people leave following the Sunday morning worship service. These heard by one minister one Sunday morning are a not unusual assortment.

"John, that was a great sermon!" "I think the choir was tremendous today, don't you?" "Reverend Edwards, the ceiling light in the ladies' room has been burned out for two weeks now." "Are the trustees supposed to meet this Tuesday night or is that next week?" "Preacher, you spoke to me right where I was this morning." "I just adore the way your two children sit so quietly all through the worship service every week. Why can't other folks teach their children to be more respectful of God's house?" "Pastor, have you any news on how Paul Zimmerman is doing since his operation?" "That was a nice crowd we had this morning, Padre; I wish we could do that well every week. It sure would help our budget!" "That was one of the best sermons you've preached since you've been here. Did you pull it out of the barrel or was that prepared especially for today?" "Pastor, I wasn't sure whether you were praying or preaching during that pastoral prayer." "It sure was good to see Mr. Adams back in his usual place, wasn't it, Pastor?"

This assortment of comments represents one form of evaluation of the corporate worship experience in many congregations. It is *not* the only evaluation, however. There are many methods used for evaluating the corporate worship experience. The most highly visible and one of the most widely used is to compare the number of members who decided to attend with the number of members who decided to stay away. Another is to listen to the content of the messages circulated on the local church grapevine.

Among the most useful questions for reviewing the system of evaluating worship in your congregation are these four:

1. What are the standards (criteria or yardsticks) used for evaluating worship here?

2. What is being done to help the people improve the quality and usefulness of these standards or yardsticks?

3. Who uses which of these standards?

4. How effective is the system in bringing the content of these evaluations to the attention of the leaders, including the minister?

One of the common and very significant characteristics of these questions is that the leaders of the congregation have some degree of control over the responses to all four. By what they do, what they do not do, and how they do it, the leaders of every congregation have a tremendous impact on the processes used to evaluate corporate worship.

A widely used method in evaluating worship is to place an evaluation card in the pew racks or to include it with the bulletin for the service. Typically this card has three to six questions on it, each one of which can be answered with a check mark. This procedure does have the disadvantage of "locking in" the respondent to the categories offered with each question, but it also facilitates the evaluation process and greatly simplifies the tabulation of the responses.

The three examples illustrate both the procedure and the content of the questions:

1. Today I found this worship service to be
   — a joyful, meaningful, uplifting, and/or helpful experience
   — a dull, lifeless, and uninspiring experience
   — somewhere in between those two.

2. Today the sermon
   — spoke directly to the concerns and questions I brought with me
   — was interesting, but not especially relevant to me
   — was neither interesting nor very helpful.

3. The most meaningful and helpful part of today's worship experience for me was (please check one):

— congregational singing

— prayers

— sermon

— confessions

— anthem or special music

— being a part of *this* worshiping community

— simply the chance to be here to worship God

— Holy Communion

— the familiar litany.

The cards are collected at the end of the worship service (a common procedure is to ask the people to drop them in a box as they leave the building) and tabulated. Occasionally the results are printed in the parish newsletter or in the bulletin for the following Sunday.

An alternative which requires more time and effort, but frequently is more meaningful and more rewarding to all involved, is the use of an evaluation committee. Typically four to eight individuals are asked to serve on a worship evaluation panel for three, four, five, or six weeks. Together they prepare an evaluation form which each will use as a guide. This form is to be filled out immediately after the worship service by each member of the panel. Later, perhaps on that same day, perhaps during an evening a couple of days later, the members of the evaluation panel meet with the pastor, using the form as an outline for their discussion, review and evaluate the worship service.

From the minister's perspective this structured discussion format is usually far more helpful and produces fewer frustrations than result from the use of anonymous pew cards. After meeting with three or four different evaluation committees the pastor also has a more informed understanding of the needs of the members and of what is especially meaningful.

The members of the evaluation panel usually find this to be an exceptionally meaningful experience. For some it is the first systematic experience they have had in reflecting on corporate worship and on the relationships between the several components of that corporate experience. Many are surprised to discover that what has little meaning for them is a very significant and often essential element of the total worship experience for others. They experience the diversity of what some of them had assumed to be a very homogeneous congregation. Many of them find corporate worship much more meaningful after serving for a few weeks on this evaluation panel. Several gain a new understanding of the responsibilities of the minister in leading a formal worship experience. For some lay persons, serving on the evaluation panel helps increase their self-confidence to the point that they feel ready to take a more active role in helping to lead in corporate worship. For many serving on the panel opens the door to other new experiences in spiritual growth.

In preparing the evaluation form to be used by the panel it may be helpful to include questions such as these:

1. How did the preacher come across to you?
   Sincere ___   Comforting ___
   Angry ___   Committed ___
   Judgmental ___   Joyful ___
   Accepting ___   Tired ___
   Condemning ___   Indifferent ___
   Challenging ___   Intellectual ___

2. How did you respond to the music?
   Positively ___   Joyously ___
   Bored ___   Negatively ___

3. What was your response to the physical setting and facilities?

Does this suggest new approaches to evaluating worship in your congregation?

What Are the Rules Here?

The fourth in this list of evaluation questions is the most subtle and the most subjective. It is also a means of identifying one of the two or three most important issues in regard to the evangelistic outreach of the church, the assimilation of newcomers, the size of the fellowship circle in comparison with the membership circle (see page 151), the factors influencing the giving level of the congregation, the process of leadership development, and the health of the group life of the congregation.

Perhaps the best way to describe this evaluation question is by a series of examples.

The clock on the dash of the compact car read 10:51 as the young couple drove into the parking lot at Trinity Church on a sunny July Sunday morning. They had moved into their new apartment the previous Thursday following his transfer from a position in another state for the same national corporation. While they were getting settled in their apartment and beginning to become acquainted with the community, they had driven past Trinity Church. Since it was the only congregation of their denomination in this suburban community, they carefully studied the bulletin board in the front yard of the church. It carried the message that the Sunday morning schedule included worship at 9:00 and 11:00 with Sunday church school at 10 A.M. They had decided to "sleep in" Sunday morning and attend the 11 A.M. worship service. As they walked from the parking lot toward the front entrance they met an older couple. "Could we help you?" inquired the white-haired man. "Yes, we were planning to worship with you this morning, but it looks as if it'll be a small crowd, or else we're earlier than we thought," replied the young husband. "Sorry, but I'm afraid you're late," was the response. "Church has been over for nearly a half-hour. In the summer, with so many people away on vacation, we just have the one service at 9:30. Are you folks new in town?" "Yes, we are," came the response as they hurried back to their car to drive back to where they had seen several cars driving into the parking lot of a Presbyterian church. They got back there in time to enter with a dozen other latecomers during the opening hymn. They happened to be seated next to another couple. At the conclusion of the worship service this young couple invited the newcomers to "come along with us to our Sunday school class picnic."

Several months later, when they were asked by an outsider, "Why are you a member of that congregation?" the young couple retold this story and concluded with the comment "And that's why, although neither of us has a Presbyterian background, we're members of this Presbyterian church today."

Stanley and Dorothy Cole came to Zion Church a few weeks after moving into town. This happened to be Communion Sunday, where the custom was for the congregation to be served while seated in the pews. As the tray with the cups was passed, each of the two visitors lifted a cup from the outer circle. As they walked out of the building to their car, Stanley said with great surprise, "They serve real wine there!" Since both of the Coles were accustomed to the use of grape juice in the Communion service, they never came back to Zion and eventually joined another congregation. Several years later they discovered, completely by accident, that the present Zion congregation was a product of a merger of two congregations, one of which used wine in the Communion service, and the other grape juice. One compromise in the merger agreement was that the cups in the outer two circles in the Communion tray would be filled with wine, and the cups in the inner circles would be filled with grape juice. A statement describing this procedure was usually printed in the bulletin on Communion Sundays, but it was squeezed out by other announcements on the Sunday the Coles visited Zion. None of the members even noticed the omission since they all knew the rules.

At Bethel Church the tradition is that every man has to serve as an usher for at least two years before he is considered for election to the office of deacon. The only exceptions to that custom that anyone can recall involved the sons of men who had served as both deacons and elders at Bethel.

At Main Street Church the Men's Bible Class is composed entirely of men who have passed their sixty-fifth birthday—and several are closer to eighty. When George Wilson, a seventy-year-old widower, moved into town to be close to his only daughter and her husband, he accompanied them to worship the first Sunday he was in town. He filled out a visitor's card and on Monday evening two men from the Men's Bible Class came to call on him. They invited him to attend the class, and the following Sunday morning at 9:30 he was greeted enthusiastically when he walked into the room it has been meeting in since 1957. Mr. Wilson began to feel a little uneasy when it appeared that the class was running well past the closing time. Finally, when he heard the organ playing the processional for the choir, he asked, "Shouldn't we be getting into church?" "Oh, no one here ever goes in there," came the reply. *"This* is *our* church." As he went home that day George Wilson realized that the rules at Main Street Church said he could either join the Men's Bible Class, which he thought he would enjoy, or worship with his daughter and son-in-law—but not both!

At North Church no one is seriously considered for election to an office in the women's organization unless (*a*) she is past forty-five years of age, (*b*) she is not employed outside the home, and (*c*) her husband is living and is an active member of the congregation.

At First Church the nominating committee is invariably composed of persons who are active members of one of the two dozen "small groups" which constitute the distinctive thrust of that congregation's member-oriented program. The result is that very rarely is anyone nominated for an important office unless that person is active in one of these small groups. This means that two-thirds of the members are almost entirely overlooked in the nominating process.

Since the late 1930s, when they began to replace the traditional series of Men's Classes and Women's Classes in the Sunday school with the formation of classes for young married couples, the doors at Woodlawn Church have gradually been closed to adults who have never married. The only remaining exception is one circle in the Women's Fellowship for "business and professional women." This circle meets in the evening and includes twenty-three women, nineteen of them over forty-five years of age. In 1939, 26 percent of the confirmed members age eighteen and over at Woodlawn Church were adults who had never married. Today, since the "rules have been changed" to close the doors on single adults, that percentage has dropped to 4 percent. (In 1973, 16 percent of the U.S. population age eighteen and over had never been married, and 8.3 percent of all men age thirty to forty-four had never married.)

There have been three major additions to the main building at Grace Church, plus the creation of a large off-street parking lot. These changes mean that (*a*) people rarely come to worship via the front doors facing the street, but rather through a rear door at the west edge of the parking lot, and (*b*) finding any room in the church is difficult for the stranger. There are no directional signs, since all the members know all the "shortcuts."

These episodes have been repeated in hundreds of congregations where "the rules of how we play the game here" are well known to all the leaders—and to most of the other members—but are not visible to guide the newcomers, visitors, and strangers.

Do these illustrations speak to your congregation? Is there a series of "rules" (customs which never have been written down and perhaps never even discussed) which may confuse the newcomer or close the door to some prospective members? Is it possible to identify some of these "rules"? Does the self-evaluation process you use uncover some of the rules? What is the process used in your congregation to change those rules which are thwarting the intentionality of the ministry of your church? Identifying and changing some of the rules may be the most important single step you can take in increasing the opportunities for expressions of creativity in church administration within the congregation.

What Happened to You?

From the perspective of the individual member the most important evaluation question can be summarized in these words: "Since you have been a member of this congregation, what has been a very meaningful or significant experience that has happened to you that might not have happened if you had not been a member of this congregation?"

Here again it is helpful to ask the date of this experience. In one congregation, for example, a group of two dozen leaders were asked this question. Nineteen of the twenty-four had no difficulty in lifting up one very important experience or meaningful event which still caused them to glow inwardly when they recalled it. Every one of these had occurred at least eleven years earlier, however, and six of the group had to dig back in their memory book at least twenty years in order to respond to the question. This led the questioner to ask himself what was happening here in recent years that might have meaning for newer members.

This set of five evaluation questions is not offered as a complete list. It is presented here primarily to suggest that any approach to creative church administration must mix several qualitative questions in with the traditional evaluations which emphasize quantitative considerations.

For Further Reading

Allen, Roland. *Missionary Methods: St. Paul's or Ours?* Grand Rapids: Eerdmans Publishing Co., 1962.

This volume was written in 1912 by an Anglican who had served as a missionary to China from 1895 to 1903. He spent much of the remaining forty-four years of his life writing on missionary principles. He told his son that this book would probably not gain much support until about 1960. He was right! Most of the support for his principles has emerged during the past fifteen years. Allen's concern was for the place and the preeminence of the Holy Spirit. The late 1960s and the 1970s have emerged as the era of the rediscovery of the Holy Spirit, and this has brought many people to a new appreciation of Allen's writings. After reading *Missionary Methods* it may be helpful to read next *The Spontaneous Expansion of the Church,* which was first published in 1927 and is both a rebuttal to the criticisms of *Missionary Methods* and a more mature attempt to describe the expansion of apostolic churches and of the hindrances which have inhibited the contemporary churches in their efforts to follow that example.

Anderson, James D. *To Come Alive!* New York: Harper & Row, 1973.

This is one of the very few books on church renewal to take seriously the institutional characteristics of the parish and to apply the insights of organization development to church administration. The second chapter, "The Church as a Social System," and the seventh chapter, "A Climate for Health," will be of great value to any church leader who has tended to conceptualize the worshiping congregation as a gathered community and has neglected the organizational characteristics and the factors which influence the health of any organization.

Banfield, Edward C. *The Unheavenly City Revisited.* Boston: Little, Brown, 1974.

This is an extensive revision and expansion of the author's famous book, *The Unheavenly City,* which was published in 1970 and led to accusations that the author was a racist, a bigot, and insensitive to the needs of the poor. Banfield challenges much of the conventional wisdom about the causes of urban problems, and this volume should be required reading for anyone who is seriously concerned about the role of the church in metropolitan areas in the 1970s and 1980s. Among the author's most significant conceptual contributions are his analysis of the radically present-oriented style of life and his distinctions among several types of poverty and several types of crime.

Berkley, George E. *The Administrative Revolution.* Englewood Cliffs, N.J.: Prentice-Hall, 1971.

This is an excellent introduction to the concept that the author describes as "The Crumbling Pyramid" and the increasing demand for a participatory style of decision-making.

Dahl, Robert A. *After the Revolution?* New Haven: Yale University Press, 1970.

Though much has been written on the subject of participatory democracy, Dahl is one of the few to tackle the question when and why we must and do delegate to others authority to make decisions which will influence our destiny. For those who are tired of reading books that describe the problem and seek one which offers "handles" for problem-solving, this is an excellent beginning!

Deasy, C. M. *Design for Human Affairs.* Cambridge, Mass.: Schenkman Publishing Co., 1974.

Only in recent years have behavioral scientists and architects begun to listen to one another (each has been talking to the other for decades), and this volume is by an architect who not only listened but also took seriously what he heard. Indirectly he explains why the building committee of 1893 or 1927 is still the most influential factor in program-planning, evangelism, and worship in hundreds of congregations. This volume should be required reading for every leader in every congregation which is considering the construction of a new building or a major remodeling of an existing structure. While he rarely speaks directly to "church problems," the book is full of helpful insights on how building design influences human behavior.

Friedman, John. *Retracking America: A Theory of Transactive Planning.* Anchor Books; Garden City, N.Y.: Doubleday & Co., 1973.

Though this is a difficult book to read, it is worth the effort. Among his major contributions are the author's distinction between the traditional allocative form of planning and innovative planning, and his learning society in which the expert and the client learn from one another.

Glasse, James D. *Putting It Together in the Parish.* Nashville: Abingdon Press, 1972.

Many ministers have been evicted from a pastorate for not paying the rent. This is only one of a score of helpful insights in the self-examination process which the author offers the reader. If this volume were required reading for every pastor in the first year following seminary graduation, it would be a better world and there would be fewer unhappy ministers in the parish ministry!

Greenleaf, Robert K. *The Servant as Leader.* Cambridge, Mass.: Center for Applied Studies, 1973.

This thirty-seven-page pamphlet is an exceptionally thoughtful and provocative essay on the role and responsibilities of anyone who accepts the role of leader and tries to practice the concept of servanthood—in other words, it is highly recommended for pastors.

Howse, W. L., and Thomason, W. O. *A Dynamic Church.* Nashville: Convention Press, 1969.

These two authors present a dynamic concept of the local church, accompanied by a comprehensive design for the many educational and ministry tasks that comprise a church's ministry design.

Jones, Ezra Earl, and Wilson, Robert L. *What's Ahead for Old First Church?* New York: Harper & Row, 1974.

While the tone fluctuates between hard realism and pessimism, this is by far the best book to offer meaningful guidance to the leaders of the downtown congregation.

Judy, Marvin T. *Multiple Staff Ministry.* Nashville: Abingdon Press, 1969.

In this very comprehensive volume the author presents findings and interpretations growing out of a massive study across denominational lines regarding multiple staff ministry and the administration thereof.

Judy, Marvin T. *The Parish Development Process.* Nashville: Abingdon Press, 1973.

Prof. Judy has devoted most of his life to cooperative ministries, and this volume represents the culmination of his experience and research in why and how to turn interchurch cooperation from a dream into reality.

Quebedeaux, Richard. *The Young Evangelicals.* New York: Harper & Row, 1974.

The leaders in the liberal and middle-of-the-road churches have become increasingly conscious of the growth of the evangelicals in American Protestantism. Many, however, are unaware of the emergence of a new and younger generation of dynamic leaders who are neither separatists nor fundamentalists, but who are mission-oriented and also exhibit a strong concern for social action. This should be required reading for anyone who carries a 1965 stereotype of evangelicalism.

Schaller, Lyle E. *Hey, That's Our Church!* Nashville: Abingdon Press, 1975.

In this volume the author attempts to demonstrate the

benefits of looking at churches by types. The problems commonly encountered by eight different types of congregations are described, and suggestions are offered on how to begin planning for a new day.

Tidwell, Charles A. *Working Together Through the Church Council.* Nashville: Convention Press, 1968.

This book suggests an approach to church ministry planning at the local congregation level comparable to that which would be done by a local church council, or a church ministry council. It deals with ministry design from the planning stage through the evaluation processes.

Wedel, Leonard E. *Building and Maintaining a Church Staff.* Nashville: Broadman Press, 1967.

This book is a comprehensive treatment of staff administration. It deals primarily with the day-by-day kinds of administrative details essential to building and maintaining an effective church staff.

Wilson, James Q. *Political Organizations.* New York: Basic Books, 1973.

This is an extremely important volume for anyone who takes seriously the concept that the institutional behavior patterns of the parish church bear many resemblances to the behavior patterns of other organizations in American life. For the person who is interested both in why people join organizations and also in which organizations they unite with—and every Christian concerned with evangelism should be interested in these questions—or any of a score of other very important questions about the relationships of people to organizations, this volume will be very helpful. Among the important questions discussed are why organizations come into existence, how organizations change, organizational democracy, leadership roles, and the formation of coalitions involving several organizations.